Spiritually Authentic

HOW TO UNLOCK YOUR SPIRITUAL GIFTS

JEMMA BROOKES

authors
AND CO.

Contents

Dedication

This book is dedicated to my two children Atlas and Ace and my rainbow child growing inside of me as I write this book.

Thank you for giving me endless purpose to do better and create a more authentic world for you to grow in. Never forget who you are and what you want. Question everything and never ever settle for less than you desire. You can have it all my darlings. I love you with everything I am.

xx

Acknowledgements

Thank you to my greatest love, my husband James, for allowing me to be who I am and accepting that my purpose comes with a lot of responsibility. You have supported me from that very first mission and never once doubted me. I am so eternally grateful for you.

Thank you to my parents for reminding me that I can do whatever I set my mind to. You have taught me how to love unconditionally and believe in myself, in turn helping me to create such an impact.

To all my clients, followers and supporters that have supported me - I wouldn't be here without you.

To all the women who came before us and who will come after, I wrote this book for you. To show you that you can be all that you are unapologetically and that your deepest sacrifices haven't been in vain. I hope to continue supporting women to embrace their gifts forevermore.

CHAPTER 1

His-story becomes her story

Do you suspect that you have spiritual abilities? Perhaps you have had unexplainable happenings and you want it confirming that you aren't imagining things? You have probably kept these experiences to yourself in fear of being judged or labelled as crazy. I totally get it. Why? Well I was the same as you.

You do not need to be any kind of way, to view yourself as 'spiritual'. The reason I feel this is so important to understand, is because of the huge misconceptions around what being spiritual actually is. The misconceptions get in the way of spiritual development by creating limiting beliefs. It could even be a false perception about spiritual connection that has been holding you back?

For as long as I can remember spirit have played an important role in my life. Without them, my life wouldn't exist. Spirit have given me a business. They gave me my husband. They've even given me children.

The most priceless gift of all, the piece that completes the puzzle, is my Spiritual Authenticity.

Without it, none of my most treasured assets would have come to fruition.

To be Authentic means '*to stay true to one's personality, spirit or character.*'

Now you may be thinking, surely being authentic is the start of your journey, but actually, it comes at the end. You will soon see how that works.

Society has been led to believe that to be a 'Spiritual person' means we have to be a vegan, tree hugging person who wears crystals in our bra and every other sentence uses the words 'divine' or 'universe'. People view those who have spiritual abilities as weird or odd. We are expected to wear purple floaty dresses and have daisies in our loosely braided hair and incense burning around our home. I have heard it all.

Then there's the other side, that being 'spiritual' means you are a 'Spiritualist'. Which means you have a religion.

Whilst I have no problem whatsoever with any of those ways of being, it is still annoying that there's always this need to have to be a particular way or fit in a certain box to prove ourselves, for being who we truly are at the core. We always seem to have a label attached to us.

I don't view myself as being religious. Nor do I have flowers in my hair or wear a bunch of amethyst bracelets on each wrist. Sometimes I forget the company I'm in and swear like a sailor. Sometimes I find myself being really 'non-spiritual' and judge others. I'm not vegan.

Although I did try being a vegetarian once when I was a teen, only to forget a month in, whilst at a friend's barbecue (that was the best hotdog ever!)

I wear the odd crystal, but I don't have this incredible collection you often see with the spiritual gurus on social media. I also much prefer candles over incense. I have good days and bad days as a mother and a wife and as a daughter and a friend.

What can I say, I'm only human?

But the point I'm making is this; you don't have to be any kind of way to see yourself as spiritual. What really matters, is how you view yourself.

It can be lonely when you come from a place of enjoying spiritual and holistic practices, or if you've had experiences with spirit. You might feel nervous about letting others know what brings you joy, or where your heart lies. You may struggle to come across like-minded souls.

Perhaps you don't have enough people in your life, you trust enough to share your experiences and beliefs with.

So what often happens, is you may turn to the internet and try to find somebody 'spiritual' that you can relate to, someone who is embracing their spiritual side. Someone who makes it seem that meditating in a meadow, amongst the sunflowers, is all you need to do to label yourself a 'spiritual woman'.

But the truth is, a lot of our 'spiritual gurus' aren't being true to themselves either. They are actually painting a picture of perfect spiritualism, which can be viewed as toxic. One that leads us to believe, in order to be considered spiritual, we must look, act and speak a certain way. This could not be further from the truth.

To be spiritual is to be AUTHENTIC.

To be able to develop your spiritual abilities, you need AUTHENTICITY.

To receive your gifts from spirit, you need to live and speak your truth. No matter how hard that is.

Then you are faced with another problem. You already think you're doing this.

But if that was true, then why are you not where you want to be in your development and awareness?

Why are you not sharing your spiritual gifts with the world?

Why when people ask you what your hobbies are, do you not immediately tell them about the spiritual and holistic practices you do?

Why do you hold back?

It's because more often than not, you will be met with a negative reaction. One of disbelief or lack of interest. I cannot tell you how many eye rolls I have had from people when I've told them what my 'job' is. But it's funny how when I relay back to them the success I've had, the amount of people I've helped, they suddenly become more inclined to want to hear more.

I'm going to teach you how to unlock your gifts and become *Spiritually Authentic*. But you have to start at the beginning. This can't be rushed.

The thing is we truly don't realise how much we absorb as children. Our parent's stories and beliefs can deeply impact us and our spiritual development. As a child our analytical brain hasn't really formed until we get to around the age of twelve years old, so what happens is we are like sponges absorbing everything.

I started life on Flintham Drive in Nottingham, on a little council estate with my mum, Tracy, dad, Alan and younger brother Dean. I have some wild memories from my first few years of life, living on that street. The craziest is probably the time we went out onto the street because of all the sirens we could hear. I remember seeing a topless man on top of a roof. There were police all at the bottom and a helicopter above and he was shouting that he wasn't coming down.

The drama. But it was always exciting, even at that age!

Mum and Dad went on to separate when I was just four years old and that was tough for me emotionally but I carried on with life. My mum met my stepdad and life was very different.

Where I was from, this was completely normal though. In fact, I didn't have a single friend whose parents *were* together. I was even considered one of the lucky ones because my dad gave up his weekend to spend time with us. So I never felt odd for that reason.

We moved from my first childhood home when I was four and into the next one on the Heathfield Estate, where my Mum still lives today. This estate was just as unpredictable, but a lot of fun was had growing up there.

We always had people around the house as I had a close group of friends and my mum loved to take care of us all. If it wasn't filled with people, it was filled with animals, from dogs to ferrets and even a squirrel once! I didn't spend much time alone. I was a very reflective child so liked to be around people to keep me from my thoughts.

Dad had to move back in with my Grandma for a while until he bought his house and we stayed with him every weekend.

It did get bitter between Mum and Dad leading up to their divorce. Dad even refused to sign the papers and had me sign them on his behalf, so they would come back as rejected.

Imagine a four year olds squiggle on the signature line.

The ten years that Mum was with my stepdad, I found myself constantly caught in the middle of Mum and Dad's feud. I hated it. I grew to love my stepdad, but was upset at myself for it at the same time. I felt I was being disloyal to my dad and for my dad loyalty was a big deal. Mum wanted us to bond but I always felt pulled, not quite knowing what I was supposed to do for the best. I was often caught in the middle.

Then there was the other side, Mum's letters. Whenever Mum needed to get something off her chest, she would write it in a letter for him. I would pass this letter to Dad and watch as he opened it and read it. On the odd occasion, I would see a tear roll down his cheek.

I have many memories of them all falling out after their separation as Mum had moved on with my stepdad Phil. I watched my ad's world fall apart and listened to his heartache. There was almost a bust up one time, but luckily Mum was able to diffuse it. I remember sitting in my car seat in the back of the car watching it escalate and feeling so concerned that I didn't know who I should be worried for. I hated always being in the middle.

I definitely took on a lot of Dad's pain in those younger years. I felt so close to him and worried about him. I came to realise as I got older, that I did that a lot as a child. I worried about Dad and Mum. I was so in tune with their energies. I was such an empath from so young, that it's only as a light worker that I understand, I was tuning into their emotions, their energy fields. I could always feel everything. Nothing seemed to be kept from me. Whether the adults realised it or not, I was aware of it all. My 'gift' started earlier than I knew.

Looking back, I get it, Dad was hurt and wanted to make life difficult for Mum. He still loved her and wished his life didn't have to change. He wanted his family to stay together. He wasn't thinking about me or how I may be construing these reactions. But Mum and Dad married young, Mum even needed permission from her parents. She was eighteen and eight months pregnant with me when they married. They both came from broken homes and wanted nothing more than to keep their own family together. But they were young. Traumatic pasts brought them together but wasn't destined to last.

I've never felt anything but immense unconditional love from both of my parents. They have been incredible and supported me through my entire existence. They weren't always aware of how they were sometimes too open with me and for that I don't blame them. The thing they weren't aware of, was that I was taking in everything I heard, saw and experienced during those years. I felt their pain alongside them. The emotional hurt they experienced, I experienced it too for them. I was empathic even at such a young age. I soon realised I could feel everything. I could sense when something was wrong. I could feel when somebody was in pain- emotionally and physically.

But how does being an empath at the age of four give clues to having spiritual abilities?

Well now, at the age of thirty-five, I am an *International Psychic Medium* and *Spiritual Mentor*. I have worked with spirit for over eleven years, translating and decoding their messages of love, support and warning. I have read for celebrities, including TV stars and helped thousands of people in countries all over the world, from Australia, USA to Saudi Arabia. I have read for doctors, nurses, teachers, members of the police force, men, women, the elderly and the young.

In these last eleven years, I have used my spiritual gifts to help people navigate and heal through the grieving process. I've guided people into creating new lives and businesses and realise their worth. I've given people the tools to start over.

For the last two years, I have taught other women how to develop their own spiritual abilities and learn to incorporate them into their everyday lives. I aligned with my purpose and am living it fully every single day.

I teach women how to live spiritually authentic in order to create a life they truly desire. The life they *deserve*. A life THEY choose using my five step system. It doesn't matter where you come from, it doesn't matter if you grew up with nothing. It doesn't matter if you didn't grow up with the type of energy that creates abundance. You can change that at any time, if you give yourself permission to be in a place of *receiving*; to get the best of what your spiritual gift has to offer.

This system isn't something that you will ever hear spoken about. In fact, if you decide to attend spiritualist churches to develop your abilities, you may be taught a process that can be considered 'out of date'. You may be faced with rules and a system that limits your progress. You may feel you are heading into a religion. You can learn the basics of connecting with your higher self-online or at a spiritualist church. But what MY system gives, is the transformation.

The transformation comes from becoming *Spiritually Authentic*. By undoing the years of blind conditioning and learning to heal from your own ancestral lineage, you can unbelievably transform your entire self and reconnect with your soul contract. Placing the power back where it rightfully belongs. Within you. Living a life on YOUR terms. Fulfilling your desires.

I believe with all of my being that this is possible for every single woman who has some level of awareness of her gift.

This is what I found.

As much as I loved to be around people who understood and believed there was life after life, I struggled to understand why spiritualism was met with so many rules. It had such an order to it.

I found spiritual churches to be very useful at the beginning of my development. But I also found the teachings they provide, can only take you so far. At times, I found the teachings to be old-fashioned and restrictive. This isn't to deflect you from joining a circle as I will always be very grateful to my mentor Ann for always encouraging me to keep going, as that was what I truly needed from my time spent there. I also found the church to be filled with incredible and friendly people always wanting to do something positive for their community. That sense of community is integral moving forward.

Sometimes I found that the very place I had come to develop and progress, was also telling me that I would not gain all I need, if I didn't do things to their particular method. With their processes, you HAD to do all of it. It was 'one size fits all'.

I also remember hearing many times that spirit will only allow you to earn so much money from your abilities, before they would cap it so you didn't get greedy.

What a way to limit your money mindset right?

I've not found this to be the case in my business. I believe we are the only ones who can put limits on our earning potential. The only thing that can stand in our way is us.

It was these reasons as to why I decided to venture out into the world of spirituality, playing to my own rules. I didn't want to be labelled a 'spiritualist' or feel kept to a particular religion. I had never classed myself as being religious before and I didn't want to start living through one now.

As much as the spiritualist church had proved to me I DID indeed have the ability to connect to spirit and my higher self, it wasn't enough. I now needed to know how far my gifts would take me. I needed to see how I could use them to create an impact. That's what was missing from the churches. There wasn't any further guidance once you had control over your connection. There weren't any steps to keep you progressing. They wanted you to unlock your abilities, but not actually go out and create a business from them. Even though, what you are unlocking was inside of you all along. It belongs to you. It is *YOUR* gift.

I decided I wanted to be able to help people, but MY WAY. As long as I always ensured our energies were protected, what was the need for such a rigid process?

I don't know if you have felt the same along the way. But I know over the years, I have had hundreds of women ask me for guidance on how to begin their spiritual awareness and development. They couldn't settle in properly in the churches, or find a place where they could really connect with others on the same path. They craved mentorship and community. They needed to feel safe whilst they learned to love and accept themselves and their gifts.

So they turned to me.

Now before I go any further, I want you to understand, I haven't always been a 'rule-breaker' or a 'rebel'. I *mostly* did as I was told as a child, I didn't like the feeling of going against the grain.

But since my awakening, I have felt very strongly against the way our society has been taught to live and I believe that my level of awareness is what draws women towards me.

I believe the limits on our spiritual development start way back to when we are a child and further limitations are added along the way.

For example - We aren't taught to be extra-ordinary.

Think about it, when do you ever remember at any point during your school life where you were taught to dream big or that it was great to be unique? Do you ever remember feeling that you and everybody in your class was unique? I don't. We were all taught exactly the same way, treated the same. We're not taught to embrace our individuality. Which is why often, we follow our peers during our education.

If we aren't encouraged to stand out from the crowd, then why would we ever want to share our unique abilities with the world? We aren't taught about the magick in the world. We are only shown how to follow a particular system, that expects us all to end up at the same place.

We were all taught the same things, the same way and expected to have the same outcome because of that.

You know - go to school, get good grades, go to university, get a job, get married and have kids. The end.

I want to show you that you can absolutely unlock your spiritual gift and claim that, without having to keep yourself in a box. Let's face it, we've pretty much spent our lives put into boxes.

These boxes give us limitations. As women we come across a lot of obstacles when attempting to put ourselves first. It just doesn't come naturally to us. We are the caregivers of the world, the ones who make sacrifices, the members of society that the rest lean on for emotional support. There is always something that keeps us from believing we can have it all.

Age- Too young or too old

You're either too young to know what you want or too old to begin chasing dreams now. You're also expected to have it all figured out from day one.

Motherhood- To be or not to be. Either way you will face judgements

Have children and you will be expected to give up your own dreams. Don't have them and you will be assumed to either be struggling to conceive or selfish.

Stay at home mum or working mum

If you stay at home, you're lazy and should be setting your children an example. Go to work- you're not being a great mum. In fact, you are being greedy, you can't have it all!

How dare a woman want more!

It's no wonder we hold back when it comes to our own needs. It's no surprise that we keep so much of how we feel inside and carry on with this mask we present to the world. But it's always been this way.

His-story tells us so.

Who are you when nobody is watching?

Do you know how to come back to yourself after a disconnection?

Are you able to access your spiritual gifts and abilities?

You need to learn how to get to know the real you. Your body and soul desire it. You will hear them talk to you throughout your time here, so you must get to know how to translate what is being put across. This is a lifelong journey, one which can totally transform your life if you are able to connect with all that is within you.

I want you to embrace all that you are and not be afraid of what others will think of that.

You are going to find out exactly how your spiritual connection can transform your entire life, just as it did mine. I created my *Five Step System* to enable all the women of the world to regain their power, to reconnect with their Ancestral History and overcome all that we have had supressing us for hundreds of years. Things that still impact us today! Including our beliefs about ourselves.

I've totally transformed from a quiet, thoughtful little girl, always with her head in a book to take her to another world, where things made more sense than here. To a lost twenty-something out of control drinker, within abusive relationships and with everything out of alignment.

To a successful business woman within the Spiritual field who has overcome many obstacles. Whilst being happily married with beautiful children and a life filled with purpose and miracles.

This *Five Step System* was all I needed to go from then to now.

CHAPTER 2

Misconceptions

I have come to realise there are many huge misconceptions surrounding spirituality, mediumship and the like.

So before I can help you understand your gifts and begin to accept them, we need to firstly pull these current outdated views apart. These misconceptions of such a wonderful birth right, are what continue to hold women back from truly connecting with their magick.

One common misconception is;

66 **You're either born gifted or you're not.** "

But this isn't the case. The truth is, we are ALL born gifted. It isn't a case of pot luck. The fact is most go on to lose touch with their gift.

There's many reasons why we go from innocent children having peculiar, unexplainable experiences to that suddenly stopping.

You see, as children, we are pure. Children are closer to light than adults. They're pure. Pure love. We haven't been on the planet long enough to be influenced or conditioned to believe in anything. So this makes our ability to communicate with spirit much stronger.

Most stories you hear of children speaking or playing with 'somebody who isn't really there' tend to be under the age of four. There's a reason for this. Children under the age of four haven't had enough influence from their surroundings, leading them to form beliefs or analyse a situation like this. They just go along with what's happening and treat it as a normal occurrence.

Now what I have found to be a typical reaction from the parent of said child is one of fear or confusion. Some parents may be terrified at the thought of their little one seeing something they can't so immediately shut it down. They may tell the child that they can't see anything or it was just a dream. Others may have had a frightening experience themselves at some point so imagine the two separate experiences as the same.

Others have a religious background and believe that communication with spirit, is really the devil's work (yes I've actually heard this one many times!)

We all want our children to reach their full potential, and we watch to identify their areas of natural strength, so that we may actively support their gifts.

We are good parents, loving parents, parents of the highest intention.

However, as parents we play a powerful role in our child's spiritual development, just as we play a powerful role in every other aspect of our child's development.

Parents can actually massively contribute towards those children losing their connection.

We turn our kids off when we:

1. Ignore their spiritual awakening, questions, and experiences. Your voice makes an experience real for your child; if a child doesn't hear a parent discussing a topic, then the child assumes that topic is not important.
2. Negative reaction- A negative statement from you about your child's spiritual experience can shut down your child's exploration because it signals to your child that his/her spiritual experiences aren't part of the parent-child connection. It can also instil fear into them due to you reacting this way. If they become afraid of what they have experienced, they will immediately shut it off. It creates a barrier type shield around this ability.

3. Discourage spiritual discovery. A negative response to your child's spiritual exploration is a lost opportunity, a moment when you could have, but didn't, support your child's vulnerable, and emerging spirituality. You don't have to agree with your child-you simply need to be interested, curious, and open to it. If you treat your child's experience as though it didn't happen, or tell them they imagined it, this can create feelings of not being heard or not being accepted. It would be very difficult for a child to continue down this path should they have this type of reaction.

It's important to be aware that old parenting and educational paradigms won't work for these kids and can delay their path. This will be the next generation. We can truly shape the future of this planet, just by being aware of our reactions to our child's spiritual experiences.

It's been proven that children who practice 'spirituality' in some form are 40% less likely to abuse substances and 60% less likely to have depression.

Another side perspective off this is that people assume that in order for you to have the gift, it has to run in the family. Again not true.

The reason people assume it's something that's generational, is that when a family are open to believing in connection to spirit, it makes it much easier for a person to accept their gifts and be open about it.

For example, I have found a lot of the Irish community discuss their gifts and we will hear of stories of a woman being open to spirit, but so was her Nan and generations before her. Therefore, it must run through the family in some way. But how it really comes to be, is if your nan was aware of her gift and was accepted within her community for being gifted, then it makes it easier for the generation after her to unlock their gifts and naturally gravitate towards sharing them. They know the acceptance is already there. They won't be met with judgement or negativity.

It was like that for me. Every Sunday whilst spending the weekend with my dad, we would go to my grandma's house for dinner. Sometimes Aunty Deborah would be there and she is a very spiritual woman. She had a way of guiding the conversation back to spiritual topics. The conversation would always come back to spirit or our ancestry. We would all pull cards at the table and discuss my great grandma, who I never met, who also had a gift. She would read tea-leaves amongst other things.

Then there was my mum's side of the family. My mum and my late great Nanny-Carla had always had strong beliefs in the after-life and we attended spiritual churches together sometimes. We would often share our experiences with one another. In fact, Nanny Carla even shared with us about her seeing an angel one night. She described in such detail about this angel, it was beautiful. I remember her telling me with tears in her eyes.

It made it really easy for me to follow my own desires and eagerness to develop spiritually. I knew I would be accepted and encouraged by my family. My family always showed such a great interest in my goings on and still do. But I know had I had the opposite experience, things would have been very different.

The most common battle with false information is this;

    Mediumship is not real; it hasn't been scientifically proven. It's fake."

This one is a big one. Probably the biggest influence on society too. This point of view is usually from the type of person who is very closed off, doesn't take risks in life and usually has a guard up day to day. They prefer to say "I believe the science" without actually researching anything.

I have come across A LOT of these folk and when I try to dig deeper with them and ask why they believe this; they never have any scientific evidence to back up their claims. Just as they say I don't. Once you're able to tap into others' energy, they're very easy to spot. They will always believe somebody in a white lab coat over anything. Even if they were to experience something for themselves.

I myself have read many articles and studies over the years and I found a common theme that would cause an experiment to ALWAYS go wrong. It was that in such studies the sceptic or scientist brought volunteers in to be read by the Psychic or Medium. Now you could say, but if somebody has the gift, then surely it doesn't matter who the test subject is. But it does!

Here's why. Should I have a sceptic come to me for a reading, they came of their own accord, they are wanting something tangible from this reading, on a personal level. They are *willing* to be read. They come because THEY want to be proven wrong, not the other way around.

But hand-picked volunteers by somebody set out to disprove the gift, are likely also volunteering to 'disprove' spiritual abilities. I think for a true experiment to take place, it should be fair and both sides should go out together and pick somebody completely random.

But my issue is this- there seems to be so many people trying to prove this point, but nobody actually trying to understand where the connection comes from.

Do I think one day there will be a fair experiment?

Nope.

Another one, that usually comes from Men, is;

> **If you're really psychic, then what are the lottery numbers?"**

This is one of those misconceptions that the ego will choose to focus on. People assume being psychic, possessing psychic tendencies or abilities, automatically means you know EVERYTHING! It's impossible to know everything. If this was really how our gifts worked, how could we possibly get through even one day? Imagine- You wake up to a million and one things racing through your mind of all the worldly events to happen that day, not just to you, but to EVERYONE.

It's really hard to explain this one to folk who think this way, so I usually choose not to bother unless their energy tells me that they actually really do want to know how it works.

We can't possibly know everything there is to know as spirit will only allow you to know what you *NEED* to know. We don't need to know the lottery numbers. We are here to live within our purpose and fulfil our soul contracts. That doesn't include winning millions of pounds! (It might for some!) But we all have lessons to learn and winning a fortune will likely deter somebody from that soul path.

Have you ever heard somebody describe Spiritual connection as wrong? I have many times.

" You shouldn't be dabbling with that witchcraft"

" It's the Devil's work"

I will never forget the time when I was running my beauty business.

One day, I had a lovely new client come to see me for a treatment. I can't remember exactly how we got on to the talk about religion but I remember her telling me she was a proud catholic. I told her I had a strong connection to spirit but was of no fixed religion. She asked if I tried to communicate with them, so reluctantly I told her I had that ability. She wasn't impressed.

As lovely as she was, she couldn't help herself in telling me how what I was doing, was actually wrong. That I wasn't communicating with spirit at all, but that it was the devil's work and he was tricking me.

Once she left, I completely laughed it off. Even though I could have taken her words offensively, I knew she meant it with good intention.

The very next day, whilst I was in my room with a client, she actually came back to the salon unannounced. She passed on a gift to my co-worker and when I came out I was greeted with, no other, then a Bible. She had actually come all the way to bring me a Bible as she felt that was what I needed.

It was one of the funniest moments of my career, but it is still something that hugely stands in the way of us really connecting with our magick. I was already deep into my journey that I took this experience with a pinch of salt. But others just stepping in, could be influenced and led to believe what they're doing is indeed wrong. It could cause them to stop.

With having a family who had similar beliefs to mine, that meant I was stronger with pushing through the forceful opinions of others. But some may have taken that personal.

There is a lot of fear around our abilities which also stem way back to the 14th century with the very first 'witch hunts'. They started in France and Switzerland and soon spread around the world.

Women were persecuted for the most insignificant of things, including using herbs to treat health conditions, or talking to the animals that crossed their paths. Some were even killed for being seen dancing in their home, without music. They were labelled witches. Women who were in communication with the devil and had sinister intentions.

So because of this time in History, a lot of people still share this generational belief that a woman who is in connection with her soul and doesn't care what people think, must be practicing some type of sorcery to bring bad to this world.

The absolute irony being that as light workers, we are here to spread love. Not evil.

Another misconception is;

" Mediums shouldn't be charging money for their gifts. "

I have strong beliefs that we are all born gifted. Some go on to put the work in to re-connect with theirs, others don't. It's as simple as that.

Just the same as if you were a good singer. You could be good and decide to really put the work in, to be the best. Or you could just let your talent fall apart, grow up to smoke and not treat your beautiful voice the way it deserves. Therefore, losing your talent.

So who decides that you shouldn't earn a living from your skills?

If you worked a corporate role and kept updating your skillset, you would gain financial reward. What's the difference? I do believe jealousy comes into this. Spiritual connection isn't viewed as a physical talent, skill or gift. Not the way the ability to paint or dance is viewed. So because it isn't seen with the human eye, it's overlooked as something not worthy.

I spent six years attending a spiritualist church on a weekly basis, paying every week to enhance my skills. I have invested a lot of money into my craft over the years. I quit my job to do this full-time.

What makes my skillset lesser than any other?

How on earth could I pay my bills if I didn't charge money for my time?

If you put the work in and commit to your craft, why shouldn't you receive a financial reward, the same as any other industry?

When I first started charging for my readings, it was a very small amount. But over the years, as my gift became stronger and I worked harder, I soon began to realise my worth and see that I should be charging more. It soon became something that would take up a lot of my time. As much, if not more, than a full time job. I had truly invested every single moment I had to be as good as I am. But nobody sees the hard work that goes into this gift. It's extremely draining physically and emotionally throughout most of it. There is so much to learn. In fact, you will always be learning.

It's really insulting how mediumship is seen as something that should be given for free. The lack of appreciation for such a wonderful gift is astounding.

From that very first day I began offering readings as a service, I loved it! I love connecting with spirit for others so much, that it doesn't feel like work at all. In the wise words of my Grandad Austin (who also ran his own business and was a workaholic);

> **If you love what you do, you will never work a day in your life."**

So when others see how content your connection makes you AND that you get paid for it, it can trigger them and cause projection. There's not many people who live to work. This brings me onto my next point...

The way Spiritual workers are played out in society.

Think of any movie or TV show and we are always portrayed as either con artists, frauds or evil.

A perfect example is the movie Ghost. This was one of my favourites as a kid. I adored how Ada Mae, played by Whoopi Goldberg, brought Sam and Molly together that one last time. But if you look at how the story began, Ada Mae was conning vulnerable people by pretending to communicate with their crossed over loved ones. You also go on to see how difficult it is for her to get Molly to believe her.

You may think 'Oh but that's just TV'. But is it? The things we see contribute and influence our belief system massively. Many, who for example, had already heard one of their parents describe Mediums as frauds, are even more likely to take on that belief as their own, without doing any kind of research into it themselves.

It seems as though we never get a fair ride. The gifts we possess have never been accepted enough, for us as women to feel comfortable sharing them or even embracing them. It's no wonder so many women keep this gift to themselves.

I often imagine a world where we are taught immediately to be ourselves. To embrace and accept all that we are. To have no 'perfect images' out there in the media, contributing massively to our overall thoughts about ourselves.

If there was less of a focus on 'perfect' and more on the 'real', we may find that the generations to come, will be more comfortable embracing their natural abilities. The young people of the world could develop their intuitive gifts right away, rather than having to disassociate with them, in fear of other's opinions and beliefs. Just imagine how life could have been had you been encouraged from a child, instead of being dismissed. Or, to be so in tune with other's energies, that you could have saved yourself a lot of heart ache in life.

It's my belief that if there was a deeper understanding about what being spiritual truly was, we would have more happiness in the world. But I'll go into that further when I tell you what step one is…

In the next chapters, I am going to introduce you to my *Five Steps to Spiritual Connection.*

CHAPTER 3

Revisit

REVISIT- TO COME BACK TO OR VISIT AGAIN

S ome may say- you should never look back, only forwards. I understand that I really do. But the reason behind this being Step One, that very first step in you achieving spiritual connection, is that it's the only way to reveal the clues.

The clues are the roots that are keeping you from reaching your fullest potential. Your past holds onto the parts of your life that you may not remember or think are relevant. Often suppressed in your deep subconscious to keep you protected. The traumas that you experienced, the cruel words or jibes once upon a time are all relevant and crucial in working through, in order to give you what you need from your spiritual development. The parts that may answer the questions you have today. This is imperative if you want to be able to develop and *use* your gift.

You will hear me say often throughout this book that spirit have given me so much. I make this point regularly because I need you to see how you too can create something so meaningful and transformational.

You could trawl the internet for information on how to develop your abilities. You can attend a spiritual circle to learn how to read energy or tarot cards for example. But, you will soon arrive at the destination I refer to, as the 'I'm not good enough Road', if you don't do this work.

You could even come to the thinking that 'manifestation' is the only way to have everything that you want. But there's something much deeper happening within us if we only awaken it.

You will take to your gift like a duck to water, but as soon as the self-doubt creeps in, it can be the end to your journey. If you follow this step, it can undo a lot of the conditioning you have become attached to, resulting in the most beautiful spiritual transformation.

The people in my life who knew me as a child, to now, have all commented on how different I am today. They've seen my ups and downs and still cannot believe that this is me today.

Today, I am confident, fearless and always inspired by so much in life. I live with an attitude of gratitude and am reminded every single day why I am on this path. I am so connected to my ancestry, nature and the soul. The only way it can be described, is transformational.

I was a quiet child, so I'm told. I learned to read aged four so always had my head in a book. I enjoyed to sing and dance and any creative activities that involved using my imagination. I had many friends, but really enjoyed being in my own company. Which always amazes people when they meet me today. I am full of confidence at the age of thirty-five and don't hold back with my passions or beliefs at all.

But I do have memories from the age of five years old where I would shy away from the spotlight.

One example of this, is a memory I recall from being five years old and being picked to play Mary in the Nativity at school. As soon as the teacher said I had to kiss the boy who was picked to play Joseph, I sat back down and refused to budge! I didn't want everybody to see me do that. I wanted so badly to play the part as I found early in life I loved to sing, dance and act. But for some reason I was not one for the spotlight. I hated any kind of attention and it showed.

Considering how I put myself out into the spotlight now, you never would have guessed.

I gravitated towards friends who were louder than me, more confident. I was able to tune into the energy of a room very quickly and understood that the more forthcoming characters seemed to be more likely to end up in a scuffle or some conflict. There was a lot of that, even in primary school. The only time I used my voice, was to defend my classmates who were picked on and not able to defend themselves. I went through my whole school life never having a single fight. The bad boys in school warmed to me and whenever something was kicking off, I either found myself being the mediator who could make them calm down, or I was able to be left alone. I had empathy by the bucket load. I had a calming energy that spoke silently to the troublesome characters, they trusted me.

Tuning into energy came so naturally to me. I could sense when something was about to happen before it did.

It wasn't until I came to do my shadow work and revisit the roots of my limiting beliefs, that I came to realise; it wasn't that I didn't like attention at all. I spent a huge part of my childhood choreographing dance routines and performing to total strangers in our garden; how could I hate attention if I could do that? The truth was that I was ok with attention, as long as I had the control.

I have come to realise that this stems from my first experience with spirit.

It all began when I was seven years old and my great Grandad Jack passed away. Although I was young, I did overhear at some point that he was very poorly. It turned out to be lung cancer. I didn't take much of that in being so young. I don't think my brother and I saw him whilst he was poorly at all.

But the day came and I remember walking through the front door, after spending the weekend at my dad's, to my mum in floods of tears, eyes all puffy. She greeted me at the doors with the words 'Grandad has gone, he's passed away.'

I couldn't understand why she was so sad. You see, at this tender age, I already accepted and knew that death did not mean the end. Death does not mean 'gone'. I'm not sure how I knew that but I just did. I could hear what she was telling me, but it just didn't provoke any reaction or emotion from me.

The incredible part though, was that I could see Grandad, clear as day right there, I could see him in spirit form.

Why was everybody so sad? He wasn't *GONE* gone.

I couldn't cry because I wasn't sad. There was nothing to be sad about, so I felt.

In fact, I remember walking straight up to my bedroom and trying my hardest to think of something sad, just so I could join in with the crying and fit in with everybody else in the house. I didn't want to be the odd one out. I almost felt like a bad person for not feeling the same way.

That night, as I was in bed beginning to fall to sleep, I was woken by my Grandad Jack's voice. I opened my eyes to see a whole scene right in front of me. He wasn't alone, he had my great Grandad Grace with him. I watched as they joked away laughing, talking. They were inside a living room that I couldn't place. But I could see the colours on the walls, it felt warm and comforting. Both of my great Grandads were sat in their own arm chairs, just as I had memories of them doing so when alive. It was as though they hadn't even noticed I was there. I felt like I had actually imposed on their catch up.

But eventually they turned towards me and they began to tell me things I wasn't aware of.

Grandad Jack told me about Mum and how I had to look out for her. He said she would need me. That she was struggling right now and going through so much and he knew she wasn't doing well. He knew she was going to miss him deeply. He said she would need me. They both told me they were proud of me and Grandad Jack smiled at me so proudly, just like he always did.

I wasn't particularly close with Grandad Grace when he was alive. I didn't spend much time around him when he was here. When I did happen to see him, he always just sounded and looked so stern and I sometimes found him a little serious. I do remember he was always telling jokes though. Maybe they were a bit more for the adults seeing as I do remember Grandma Grace always telling him off!

In her squeaky voice- "Ooh Geoff pack it in!"

I told my mum the very next morning what had happened, and her reaction was a mixture of pure happiness and also a hint of *'wow did this actually happen?'*.

I think even then I was a little worried I wouldn't be believed. I never once questioned what I had experienced, I never wondered what it all meant, it felt so natural. But it wasn't something that I had heard anybody else share. I was pretty sure I was the only one who had seen them both since they apparently 'left us'.

To be honest, I probably would have kept it a secret and to myself if it hadn't been for Grandad talking about Mum. I knew I had to tell her because I knew it would bring her some peace. She couldn't believe the message. It all made so much sense to her.

Mum began to cry, but I sensed it was happy tears, tears that represented her feeling overwhelmed. I knew telling her was the right thing to do, so she knew that he hadn't really gone. He was still present, in some form.

Looking back, maybe I was supposed to tell her, in order to bring my gift to light. She definitely didn't let me forget about what happened, even years later!

As I got older and it was brought up once, she told me what that message really meant to her and it really did hit home. With me being only seven at the time, a lot of what

Grandad had said sounded like riddles to me. I wasn't aware of how much Mum was really going through at the time of his death, her relationship with my step-dad was falling apart.

My mum was very excited about my experience that she began calling Fanfan (that's what I call my nan) immediately to relay it all to her. Everyone we bumped in to, she would put me on the spot and ask me to repeat it again word for word. It soon put a stop to me wanting to share my experiences with others.

She didn't realise at the time, but this was a lot for a child to take in. Mostly because of the unwanted attention I was receiving. I didn't like being asked all the time about it.

It felt personal and private.

Sacred even.

Or at least it did before everybody knew about it.

What Mum didn't realise, which most parents don't, is that I became very aware that I was different at this point. Although the initial reaction from Mum was positive and accepting, the fact that I had to tell everyone about it, proved to me that this wasn't typical of others to be doing. It was very obvious that what had happened wasn't normal. I felt odd and I didn't like it.

See what I didn't share with anybody else was that seeing my Grandads wasn't the only unexplainable experience I had had.

I spent many nights when drifting off to sleep, almost pulling myself out of my body. I would often open my eyes and look down at my sleeping body. It was incredible.

I could do this whenever I pleased. If I got into bed and wasn't feeling very tired, I would lay there and decide where I wanted to go. Most times I would take myself to the park over the road. I would fly over there, really high above it all. I could see for miles.

As a child I thought this was magic.

I thought I was magic.

But now I know, that this was what we refer to as *Astral Travelling*. I did this whenever I felt like it. I decided to keep this to myself after as I knew it would no longer feel like mine if I was to share it.

I never told a single soul about my midnight travels. I would continue doing this up until around the age of eleven or so. Until my bedtime routine changed. I was now experiencing 'big school' problems. Hormones, exams and social stresses soon knocked my spiritual dedication right out of me! This only got worse as I went into my teens.

As I told you that there are many of us who begin this

journey with such abilities, there are also many of us who lose our way. A lot of us veer off down a different path and lose sight of our gifts.

Including me.

I lost touch with my connection through traumatic experiences I had throughout life.

As a woman, you are created with your psyche deep down inside of you. It is your secret weapon in life. It tells you all you know and all you are yet to know. It is the curiosity within you. It is the gut feeling when something doesn't feel right. Without this knowing, you are without proper protection. Your mind, body and spirit suffer.

To have this birth right taken from you, to strip a woman of her intuitive nature, is taking away her perception. Your conscious knowledge becomes nothingness.

This happened to me. Time and time again.

I met my first boyfriend at fifteen and he wasn't just your typical 'bad boy'.

He was much worse than that.

He was a drug taking, drug dealing, compulsive liar who preyed on underage girls. A thief, a sexual abuser, and he had many enemies.

During that three-and-a-half-year relationship, I learned a lot and I lost a lot. I grew up quicker than I should have had to. That relationship put me in many dangerous situations which still to this day can trigger me if I watch something similar on TV or hear a story about someone.

It was this relationship that killed my psyche. Literally ripped it from right out of my body. This was a relationship that started with lies and ended just the same way. I was naïve and pure at the beginning, but by the end, an argumentative and angry woman. I was taken advantage of, abused mentally and sexually. Resulting in me no longer recognising who I was. I had lost my essence. Everything I was up until that relationship was fading away.

I lost friends as not many liked him. My school friends stayed on at sixth form, whereas I was manipulated into going to college instead.

My friends from the estate didn't like him and with his efforts, we drifted apart. I became accustomed to being in the company of his crowd who were drug dealers, thieves and just ugly hearted people.

My parents hated him, which escalated to full blown arguments between him and my mum. It was also the first time Mum and I began to fall out. We had always been best friends. Mum had me at only eighteen, there was nothing that we didn't share, we were always extremely close. I've always been her rock, as she had been mine. But he came between that.

I had never had such conflict in my life. Everybody was against me thanks to him. The girls from the estate knew about his deceptions so laughed at me. The boys were too afraid to tell me what was going on as he had physically assaulted one boy for even looking at me.

I couldn't talk about my traumas to anyone. Nobody would be willing to just hear me. I would only be told that I needed to leave. Which wasn't what I wanted to hear. I was barely happy during that time, but I wasn't someone who just gave up on things. With him being my first proper boyfriend, I couldn't just walk away without a good enough reason; that being that I needed to have proof of infidelity.

Every time a rumour arrived at my door, I would confront him. He denied it of course. He would tell me I was crazy. But I just had this inner knowing that there was truth in these stories. This was my biggest battle during this time. Knowing when I was right with my psyche and when I was wrong.

Even if I didn't have any solid proof, I just knew. But lie after lie, tears after tears, I lost more and more of my intuition.

Looking back now, I can pinpoint that exact moment when it had gone.

He had gone on one of his many disappearing acts. He didn't have a mobile phone back then and I couldn't drive, so I would have to go searching myself on foot all around the places I could maybe find him.

Well this one time, it just wasn't working and even Mum came to help me. We were both getting worried as it had been a few days.

Eventually, he rang me from a phone box.

He was in tears so I was seriously worried. He began to explain to me why he had gone AWOL.

He told me he had discovered he had cancer.

I couldn't believe what I was hearing! My heart was breaking as I listened to his words. He sounded terrified. He didn't want to burden me with it all so he fled instead. He told me he had been staying at his cousin's home on the sofa going over everything. He had been missing because he didn't know how he was going to break this awful news to me.

I was devastated. Heartbroken.

I came off the phone and told my Mum. She was livid. In fact, she hit the roof.

I was not expecting such a huge reaction. She told me I was stupid to believe such nonsense, that he is most certainly lying again. She began asking me loads of questions about his diagnosis and how it had all come about. I couldn't believe she would think that he could possibly make something like this up. Sure, he had lied about everything else before, but surely not something as huge as this.

How could anybody lie about something so awful?

We met up and I held onto him so tightly. I was so frightened at what the future held for us now. But it wasn't long before things got back on track. I decided to keep him away from the house to avoid more fights.

I met him every Friday (when I wasn't at college or working at my retail job) outside the cancer unit at the hospital. He would tell me how awful his treatment had been and I would do my best to take care of him that evening. He certainly didn't look very well. He always had a slight greyish tone to his skin.

I was only seventeen, taking on such a devastating verdict. He seemed to carry on with his usual activities though. He didn't seem particularly tired or poorly. He seemed pretty much the same as he always had done.

Eventually it all unravelled.

He had lied about having cancer.

The whole thing was a complete web of lies. A story he had concocted in order to keep me from leaving him for what he had actually been up to during those few days he went missing.

Our council estate's equivalent to;

" **Sex, Drugs, Rock and Roll'**

I ended the relationship. Briefly.

Looking back, I realise that I had lost touch with all that was within me. I was having out of body experiences. I was a lost soul. My intuition had become stained and my perception clouded. Everybody could see what was happening but me.

I had become intuitively blind.

My mum put it to me once like this:

"You are in a bubble Jem. We are all on the outside willing you to see what's going on, but you can't. Please step out of that bubble and look at yourself. Please see what we can see."

There was a lot wrong with this person but I just wanted to fix him. In trying to do this, I broke myself. My spirit was shattered. I had no clue what was real and what was in my head. I had no intuition left. I stopped sensing spirit around me. I stopped doing the things I loved, such as reading and dancing. I had no sense of purpose and was losing my sense of reality.

How could I ever get it back? How could I find myself?

Such a traumatic relationship, at such an impressionable

age, led me to suffer emotionally and mentally for the next few years after it had all ended. It was at the end of my next relationship that I 're-connected' back to my soul level.

During that relationship, new habits had formed. I no longer chose happiness. I allowed my entire focus to be on him. This gave him my power. The person I was at the beginning no longer existed, instead he had created me a new identity.

If you hear something said about yourself enough, you can go on to form an identity around it. For example- with all that I experienced with this person, he would often tell me I was crazy. I was imagining things in my head. I had no proof. So eventually, I began to accept that. I no longer paid attention to my intuition, my spiritual connection, my 'inner-knowing'. If anything, it was haunting me.

I decided my intuition was sending me crazy. That made more sense, than to believe I was being manipulated or abused. That inner knowing was driving me crazy, with the constant 'not knowing.' I doubted every feeling, thought or instinct I had. Even if I briefly went with it, I soon put it to the side in favour of 'physical evidence' of wrong doing.

Whenever I tried to voice my feelings or hurt, I wasn't listened to.

This led to me being a person who kept things to herself.

It gave me the thought process that *my voice wasn't one people wanted to listen to.* My voice, feelings and needs were irrelevant. They didn't matter.

I soon created a belief around that.

Which is one of the main reasons it took me over three years to hold my first show with an audience!

We are losing more and more of our natural abilities, our natural connections to the planet and source. There are many ways to limit your spiritual development. Including your belief system.

Your entire history is based on a set of beliefs you have had your whole life.

From the ages of four to twelve is when you create your first set of beliefs. Your beliefs around money, relationships, career and even the way you think about yourself all start as a story you tell yourself.

For example- Let's say you grew up in a home where Mum stayed at home to raise the children and Dad went out to work. Mum's always ran off her feet taking care of everything and you rarely see Dad as he has to provide for his family. Perhaps you hear about a new game that all your friends are getting. You tell your dad you would like it too. But the answer you get is, "We're not made of money".

You go to the supermarket and ask to have the magazine

that comes with the toy, but are met with, "Money doesn't grow on trees you know!"

Then you often hear Mum and Dad arguing about money. They never seem to have enough and your mum would like to see more of Dad but he has to work extra hours to bring in the money as costs keep rising.

If this was your reality, then you will likely grow to have a difficult relationship with money. I did. When you consistently hear things like this growing up, you are likely to come from a place of lack as an adult. You may be stingy with spending money, always worried about not having enough to make it through the month. You may feel like you are always chasing that end of the month pay check. Or you may have the same mind-set I had growing up.

That was to repel money.

I associated money with problems and conflict as I always saw my parents fall out about it. Even growing into an adult, it was still the number one fallout amongst family members.

Whether it be people falling out over money borrowed, or an inheritance that wasn't shared fairly.

So once I began making my own, I spent it within a few days of getting it.

It's like it burned a hole in my pocket!

So as a working adult, I had no care for money, it didn't motivate me and I didn't want it. I had zero savings, an overdrawn overdraft and always came from a place of lack. I saw how money got in between relationships and caused drama. So subconsciously, as soon as I had some, I got rid.

But you see, had my story around money been more positive as a child, this could have meant that I had an entirely different attitude towards it, once I became independent to make my own.

If your belief system around your confidence or spirituality has been a negative or difficult one, then you are going to need to re-write your story. If you have experienced a traumatic event or relationship, this may have contributed massively to your connection. You will need to dig deep to look at anything from your past that may have caused you to have a block.

As you see, for me, my intuition was described as a 'crazy thought'. Nothing more. I was laughed at by those who knew I was right all along. But made to feel that I had got it so wrong. I began to despair my gift. No longer was it sacred or special. It was a burden that I needed to silence.

I meet many women who have incredible connection and the ability to change the world with their gifts, but their limiting beliefs completely hold them back. Many of them have feelings of being a fraud because they completely lack confidence, so then the self-doubt creeps in and takes over. Often this comes from somewhere in their younger years they were made to feel 'less than'.

For example, you may have shared an experience you had with a group of friends but then somebody outright laughed at you and called you a liar. You are then asked to prove your experience. This kind of situation is so common amongst us spiritual women. We are often asked to prove what we experience, but if we were to tell a story of achieving something or witnessing something terrible, we wouldn't receive such a reaction. From then on, you'd probably keep your spiritual happenings to yourself in fear or the embarrassment felt from this experience.

Or maybe you are certain of your gift, you proudly share it with your close ones, but every time somebody tells you that you should put your gift to good use and maybe start a business or read for members of the public, you freeze up. That inner voice in your head tells you that you aren't good enough, or experienced enough to put yourself forward like that.

So you continue down a path of keeping yourself small.

Yet if you looked back, you may recall a memory of sharing a personal achievement proudly with your parent, only to be left feeling like they didn't really acknowledge it. Then made to feel like you should have done better.

Can you relate to this? You know you have a gift; you've had experiences you can't explain.

You sometimes just *know* things. But a little voice inside begins to tell you that you aren't experienced enough. Or 'why would anybody listen to you?'

It's a defence mechanism designed to keep you safe, to protect you.

Which is great.

If what you actually heard was true.

But it isn't.

Limiting beliefs aren't true. They aren't facts.

They are formed from experiences you have either had, saw or heard growing up. They aren't designed to benefit you. In fact, they can cost you a great deal, for example: my very first day of senior school didn't start well at all. It haunted me and created one of my biggest obstacles in my career.

I went to my first class and sat on the back row, which looking back was pretty silly considering I had hearing problems. But anyway, the teacher began the register and calling out names in alphabetical order.

She came to my name and I said, 'Yes Miss' like the others before me had. But something was wrong. She told me to stand.

I immediately felt my cheeks burning as I knew they must be glowing red by now. She asked me why everybody else was wearing the correct uniform but I wasn't. She wanted to know why I wasn't wearing a tie.

I explained awkwardly that I didn't have one as I didn't know I needed to wear one. She proceeded to tell me I must have one for the next day or I'd be in trouble. Everybody had turned to look at me whilst this was happening. Thirty faces all looking at me grinning or laughing. It was the most humiliating moment for me. I wanted the ground to swallow me up.

From that day on, I could not bear the thought of standing in front of people and speaking. My fear of public speaking had begun. I was eleven years old and avoided any kind of public speaking throughout school, college and work. It was as simple as that.

The problem I faced as an adult with this was that once I had become established in my career, I really wanted to have my own shows. Shows where I could stand in front of an audience and give readings to those I felt drawn to. I wanted to be able to show so many people that spirit were with them and I could prove that to them. But this wasn't possible with such a huge fear standing in my way. One incident at the age of eleven years old was limiting my potential at the age of twenty-seven.

I just didn't want to experience that humiliation again.

For three years, I had this goal on my list of things to achieve. I just couldn't bring myself to do it. Eventually, I sat and came to the realisation that if I continued to hold myself back like this, I would never progress in the way I wanted to. My limiting belief had cost me three years of stunted progress in my career.

I genuinely thought that nobody would come to my show. Why would they? I was a nobody! I wasn't anything special. I was the same as everyone else. I just had a spiritual gift that was all.

I was so fearful of shouting about an event of my very own and risk having nobody show up. It was terrifying.

I believed that people would laugh at me, just like they did in that moment at school. I didn't believe I was good enough that people would listen to me. I'd never had a voice. I was always overpowered by bigger and louder characters. I certainly didn't exude confidence.

But none of this was true. It was just a story I had created in my mind. So I took action and hosted my own show.

Would you believe it? It was a sell-out!

I received a round of applause at the end and lots of my guests even asked when my next show would happen as they wanted to come back!

It couldn't have gone better. Even if I was shaking like a leaf the entire time! I had actually stepped outside of my comfort zone and done it! This was my proudest moment! It had led to me now hosting shows in venues that hold over 120 people and they sell-out every single time! I now need bigger venues!

By conquering my limiting belief, I have opened many other doors of opportunities to come my way. I had let my fear take over my life for way too long. For many years, I had cared about what others thought, more than my own desires.

If you were to think about how your own experiences and limiting beliefs, can you see how they are holding you back?

Go back to when you were a child. What did you see? What did you hear? What did you experience?

You may feel that it's not just your spiritual development that's keeping you stuck, but in actual fact, you may be struggling with a lack of confidence. Or even self-worth.

If you have experienced times as a child where you felt you weren't listened to, or you felt you weren't good enough, this will totally restrict your connection. If you don't feel good enough, you won't be willing to put yourself out there, take a chance and believe in yourself.

I honestly believe one of the most difficult parts of becoming Spiritually Authentic, was to unravel the clues from my past. The awareness it brought me changed my life. It will be difficult to stop listening to other's thoughts of you, or opinions on what you do, but it will change your life.

How many other women must there be with such an incredible gift, who would love to share it with the world, but are just too afraid at how they will be perceived?

There are too many to count!

Our belief system contributes to every part of our life. So you will likely see the domino effect it has, once you begin working on the limiting beliefs.

Think of the life you *could* lead, if you changed your story. If you were to re-write your script. Changing your mind-set to one of self-belief and courage will dramatically impact your spiritual development. I have witnessed it time and time again with my own students.

The moment you take full responsibility for your life is when the pieces just fit together and your messages from spirit become so much clearer. The alignment this creates within you leads to so much good. This was the first step I took and it transformed my entire life. I found my messages became clearer, so I listened easier. This meant I was able to decide what I wanted.

Life isn't happening to you.

You are the creator.

Your mind-set has to change in order to strengthen your connection with spirit and all that magick.

Throughout this book, you are going to go through an inner journey of self-discovery and reconnection. Allow yourself to feel into it all in order to trust and embrace your spiritual journey. This is your time, no more ignoring your abilities, no more never getting round to delving deeper. I want you to use this opportunity to put yourself first. Something led you to me, and I believe;

66 **When the student is ready, the teacher will appear.**"

CHAPTER 4

Recover

RECOVER- FIND OR REGAIN POSSESSION OF
SOMETHING STOLEN OR LOST

T he fourth step is Recover. This is when you recover your gift, your abilities and awareness. You find them and bring them back to the surface. They're always there, you just need to remember them.

PART ONE - THE BREAKDOWN

I had finally ended that awful relationship for good, but quickly moved into another toxic relationship. I just wasn't ready to be moving on, but somehow here I was. I needed to be on my own, reconnecting with who I was, but still was giving that very last piece of me away yet again.

I was still massively in pain about the trauma from my last relationship and I couldn't trust another man so soon. I still wasn't being met by anyone emotionally and it was finally taking a mental and physical toll on my health.

I had finally reached rock bottom. The place that so many talk about. This had become my reality.

I was done.

I was a shell of my former self. I had been signed off from work by my GP as I had decided to stop eating. It sounds funny describing it that way, as at the time, I didn't view myself to have an eating disorder because I wasn't refusing food to stay slim or to have the perfect image. I just decided to stop eating.

I had lost full control of my life and no longer knew who I was, so to try to stop everything from hurting, I took control in the form of my relationship with food.

I went into a real deep low and just stopped as easily as that. I refused all food and drank fizzy pop to keep me going.

My loved ones were devastated and crying constantly. I had given up. I no longer wanted to be on this planet living this confusing life. I was struggling to see past the hurt I felt. What was the point in being here now when I had lost so much? I had nothing left and couldn't even consider the thought of being in this kind of pain again.

I was taken to visit a therapist, which didn't make any difference. She asked me outright why I was where I was, what was hurting me. So as direct as she was, I told her about the sexual abuse with a black and white approach, just as she had. She didn't seem fazed, most definitely lacked empathy. I don't know what reaction I was expecting, or if I even had any expectations.

I remember thinking *"Well what now then?"*

Wasn't she supposed to give me the answers?

Nope. She did give me a sheet of paper with a list of helplines to call though.

I then began with OCD tendencies, such as my Arithmomania. I would sit and pull my eyelashes out and the hairs from my legs. These things made me feel so much better. Like I finally had control over something.

I eventually became so weak that I was beginning to not get off the sofa. I was under eight stone by this point as I was losing weight very quickly. Then one day, I remember Mum and Dad sitting next to me, holding my hand and pleading with me to eat something. They wanted me to just try. I had gone so long without food that just putting something in my mouth made me wretch.

But as I looked into their eyes, I could hear a voice telling me not to give up. I felt my ears stand to a point and freeze. I was desperate to hear more from this voice. I closed my eyes after a while and slept and as I did, I remember dreaming about my brother and I playing as kids. We were running about the garden laughing and smiling. I was so happy and free. In this dream, I heard that same voice again. It was telling me to keep fighting. I had to get through this and I would.

I knew that this was a voice from the spirit world as soon as it connected with me. I feel looking back now, that it was a spirit guide supporting me through this breakdown.

I woke after that sleep determined not to put my family through anymore heartache ever again. I asked my mum for some food and she was delighted! After a bit of heaving, I managed a few mouthfuls of mashed potato (one of my favourites). From then on, I began to get better. I decided to get better. I wanted to try life again.

Maybe this time on my own terms.

During that time of my life, it wasn't professionals within the system that changed my life or helped me in any way. It was my spiritual connection. It was that voice bringing forth the realisation that there were only two options- to die or to fight on.

I believe, had somebody provided holistic healing in some form, I would have been much more motivated to want to get better.

Holistic approaches such as meditation, yoga and dance help to effectively re-organize and re-process the trauma effectively through accessing the brain, mind and body. It combines the mental and emotional health with the spiritual experience.

Since the pandemic, the wellness and meditation sector has grown by 25%.

65% of people are now adopting new habits of wellness into their daily routines.

More and more people are beginning to look back to their roots and uncover the very magick they hold within. We are programmed to reach for something outside of us to fix the problem before laying the foundations of a healthier mind, body and soul.

One of the biggest hurdles we face is breaking down the conditioning of many generations of our own families. If our own parents are uneducated or ignorant to exploring alternative therapies or healing, then how are we going to be able to help ourselves through our own traumas?

If this were to begin as children, we would change so much by having all the tools we need, to not only survive certain experiences, but also to heal from them.

In one study, it was reported that:

> *by teaching mindfulness in the classroom, you can help improve students' response to stress and reduce their overall stress levels."*

> *Teachers reported a 14% increase in students' positive behaviours after the program and an 18% decrease in students' problem behaviours.*"

> *Emerging evidence indicates that alternative medicine therapies may help children to reduce symptoms for a wide range of mental health issues, including ADHD/ADD, autism, anxiety, depression, and stress.*"

For instance, many studies have suggested mindfulness-based practices (e.g., yoga, tai chi, qigong, and meditation) may be a beneficial adjunct to the treatment of mental health problems, particularly mood and anxiety disorders [29–32]. Evidence also suggest that herbal supplements and natural products (e.g., St. John's Wort, Ginkgo, Biloba, Ginseng, and Lemon Balm) can serve as promising therapeutics for childhood stress, anxiety, and depression, and help children with ADHD in reducing the difficulties of concentration and hyperactivity [24, 33, 34]. Moreover, some recent systematic reviews and meta-analyses have also demonstrated Alternative therapies can reduce mental health symptoms, such as anxiety, depression, and chronic stress, and improving quality of life [35–38]."[1]

PART TWO - THE BREAKTHROUGH

After my break-down at twenty-one, came my break-through - my awakening. I didn't return to my sales job and received a letter a week later to tell me I had in fact, been sacked. Oh well.

I kept away from men and decided to just have some fun, so that I could find myself and decide who I wanted to be.

For six months I had been single when I decided that I was ready to meet somebody. I had been going out most nights of the week for the previous six months, with friends and was beginning to crave change.

So on this particular Saturday, I declared to my friend that I was going to make it my mission that night, to meet a guy. I wasn't planning on anything too serious, I just felt ready to get to know somebody new.

We were going out for dinner on the run up to the night ahead and as we were getting ready, I noticed my Mum was reading the newspaper, so I asked her to turn to the horoscopes for me.

Mine said, *"You will find love where you see a wedding celebration"*.

I was excited. Never before had I read my horoscope and believed it, like I did this time. A sceptic would say that horoscopes are so broad that they will always be accurate for some. I agree. I prefer to analyse a whole birth chart, rather than just focus on the sun sign.

But this was just a bit of fun. A happy distraction. Even though it did feel a little synchronistic.

We went to a Chinese buffet place in the city centre and as we were eating, we heard a big crash. Looking out the window I saw a wedding car had crashed into somebody.

Something clicked!

> *You will find love where you see a wedding celebration.*"

Why did I feel so certain that this really was going to happen?

That night, we headed to our usual spot where I loved to dance and felt very comfortable. We got our drinks and headed over to the DJ booth to say 'Hi' and I just happened to notice a group of guys sat to the left of us. One in particular, I had noticed before.

For the past few weeks, just as I was leaving this bar, this very guy was just arriving. We had exchanged eye contact, but nothing more. He was definitely my type with regards to the mean and moody look he had going on. But he never smiled, didn't show much keenness, which was what I preferred.

So I decided now was the time to keep to my word. I sent my friend over to get his name and number.

It worked.

To cut a long story short - I developed some mighty courage out of nowhere that night and asked the DJ to publicly declare that I wanted him to ask me out on a date. He happily obliged. Then to make sure he wasn't going to be another terrible match for me, I sneakily found out his star sign. As it turned out, he was the perfect match to mine!

I married this man.

We have been together thirteen years and married for two. He has been my most constant person and I know that my spiritual connection brought us together. My psychic ability took heed of my horoscope and my inner knowing led me to take inspired action. It wasn't all down to spirit, but had I not embraced who I was and the things I love, regardless of what anybody else thinks, I wouldn't have taken that chance that night. I had never done anything like this before. I would never have been brazen enough to approach a man. My love for star signs since the age of seven years old, brought me my *Happy Ever After*.

I wasn't ashamed for checking my horoscope that day. I was stepping into who I was and taking on a soul-led life. Not one that satisfied others, or was typical or 'right for a woman'.

So many things can happen in your life that are unexplainable. Like when you gravitate towards certain people, but not others. Or when you want something to happen so badly, that when you're just about to give up, it comes along. Some say there is so much magick in the world, it's all a part of divine timing. But I need you to understand, that's it's you that brings the magic. *You* are the magick.

Your journey requires you to trust. Trust in the divine timing. Trust yourself. The magick in your life will become so obvious to you, once you place your trust in it. So trust it is within and you will notice it more and more.

Should you find yourself wanting to try something that wouldn't normally be something you would do- ask yourself, what's holding you back?

I was twenty-four years old when I believe I feel I fully recovered my gift. It sounds funny to say that, but that's my perception of things. My gift was once lost, but then I found it. It came back. I know many women feel this same way too.

Obviously something was there to bring me my James. Something deep inside was beginning to rise back to the surface. My psyche was coming back and the powers of this were becoming apparent to me.

But I still wasn't ready to fully embrace it until I was twenty-four. I had to *heal* first. Healing is a lengthy process sometimes. Just because I had found real love and was very happy, didn't mean I had healed from my past. But upon focusing on doing that, it is what helped me to **recover** my psyche.

It came about when I wanted to spend more time with my dad. So we began attending a local spiritualist church together on a Tuesday evening. I would come home from work and he would pick me up. We would go to the service.

A "service" is where a Medium stands in front of the audience and gives messages from spirit.

I loved it! It wasn't the environment or the people, but listening to the messages people received, seeing the tears of happiness and relief from those who connected with their loved ones. I was amazed hearing some of the messages passed on.

For the first time in my life, I was beginning to really want something.

Something that had a *purpose* behind it.

I wished I could understand my gift enough to be able to do the same. I seemed to be picked out most weeks and given a message. Every time, the Medium would tell me that they could see me stood up there. In their third eye they were being shown *little old me* standing on the stage giving meaningful evidence of spirit to those who had lost loved ones.

I was flattered and excited at the same time!

A few weeks went by when I decided to enquire with the president of the church about their development classes. She told me that anybody could join. So Dad and I did the following week. I found it unusual and fairly awkward too. We would sit in a circle and start with an opening prayer, where we would hold hands and ask spirit to allow us to work with them. It took me a long time to be comfortable with this as I didn't like holding hands with a stranger and still had some OCD tendencies around germs.

I also didn't enjoy the opening prayer as I wasn't religious and had never done a prayer before, so this felt very out of place for me. Speaking to God felt strange. I didn't *not* believe in God, but I also was unable to say I did. I was somewhere in the middle.

It took some getting used to with the meditations too. I had never done it before and found it hard to switch off. I would wonder if this was all made up and that we weren't actually connecting with anything, but instead imagining it.

I believe these are normal responses to the early stages of spiritual development. I have had many students experience the same. I sense a big part of our hesitance to believe it is actually real is down to the patriarchal ways of society and how we have been programmed to believe that if it isn't "proven" then it's not possible.

It takes some practice and commitment to establish comfortable ability with meditation. But once it's there, you soon become an expert at drifting in and out at the most unexpected times. I can go into meditation as somebody is talking to me! (Not that they would know!)

Your first step into connection is to learn how to trust when spirit connect with you. Now what I mean by this is, when I was starting out on my path I didn't know how to trust the impulses I had- the things I saw, the feelings I got. I would hold onto those feelings and go get a reading. The readings always validated what I was feeling helping strengthen the relationship with my intuition. This would prove to me that whatever it was that I felt, or saw or heard was in fact psychic ability.

Top Tip

Should you find yourself having random thoughts about things you weren't previously thinking about, write them down. Often the way spirit will tune in is to drop in random things. These things will literally appear out of the blue, into your mind's eye. It could be a message from spirit, it could be a clue as to something that is about to happen. Don't be quick to dismiss it.

It was also at the age of twenty-four, whilst I was working as a temp in a corporate role, that I went to my first Tarot Reading.

I had been in this job for a year and a half. I hated the work itself but enjoyed the team I worked with. I even met my best friend there on our very first day. But I knew I wasn't going to last there. I had no focus and I still believe the only reason I wasn't sacked was because of how I would boost the team morale. I was the 'fun' co-worker. The one who took none of it seriously. This job most definitely was not going to change my life. I had had ten jobs by this point and had worked in everything from retail to sales to finance. None of it made any sense to me. I didn't want to sit in an office or work in a shop. I couldn't take orders from anyone, that had become very apparent. I needed to work on my own terms. I wanted to make a difference but I just needed to figure out the how.

So when one of my best friends invited me along to her mum's pub for this Tarot night, I was all for it! I was desperate to know how my life was going to change. So off I went.

I honestly can't remember 99% of that reading, not because it wasn't any good. But because the first thing that reader said to me, stopped me in my tracks and I couldn't hear a word after it. She told me these words:

> *Whatever it is you are thinking of doing career-wise-do it! You will not look back! It is risky so others will tell you, but it will pay off in the long run and you will work spiritually because you have the gift!"*

Bingo!

She had hit the nail on the head!

All of a sudden, as she said those words, I just *knew* I needed to work for myself! I didn't know what to do yet, but that was the only answer, I had to do it!

The very next day, I walked into the office and handed over a hand written letter declaring my fourteen-day notice had begun. I was officially leaving this job. Everybody asked me what my plans were but all I could tell them was that I had fourteen days to figure it out.

I decided that I was going to start my own business, during a recession in 2011 and I had two weeks to figure out what that business would be…

I was beginning to get quite used to this daring and courageous version of me!

I decided to use my college qualification, which was in Beauty Therapy. Salons were doing well at the time due to

Reality TV taking over our evenings so I figured it was a good route to take.

I came across a salon that was only just opening. It was called Butterfly Hair Design. I didn't hesitate. I always had a huge connection to butterflies so took it as a sign that this was the salon I would run my beauty business from. My mind was made up.

Business was slow, for a long time. Being honest, as much as I loved to do beauty treatments and learn new skills, I still wasn't putting in enough effort. Something was still missing! I enjoyed pleasing customers whilst giving them treatments. I loved the chit chat and finding out so much about them. But I still wasn't satisfied and found myself learning new things, adding in new treatments along the way.

This is a huge sign that you are heading down the path of enlightenment. Should you find that you are eager to learn new things, perhaps heading down the path of self-improvement, this can be a tell-tale sign that your third eye is awakening and strengthening.

All the while, I was still attending the spiritualist church and I had got really good at providing evidence of life after life. I was giving readings every single session and was even being chosen to help to train newcomers when they attended. I was really beginning to find my place with my abilities. I was trusting more and more that what I had was real.

I was practising all the time. Whenever I wasn't at work, I was practising on anybody who would let me. I would seek out groups online to practise, I would ask friends if their friends would allow me to read for them. I lived and breathed it. I had fallen so deeply in love with my abilities that I began to realise that I needed to follow this path properly. I couldn't just practise and enjoy it. I felt that there was something more I should be doing. Something that would make a difference.

I started to take my Tarot cards with me to the salon and in between treating clients to facials and massages, I would be sat at my beauty couch practicing some more. I would pull cards for anyone and everyone, even celebrities.

It was then when I received my first 'business download.'

A download is when spirit drop in with an incredible message about an idea you should turn into reality. It will come out of nowhere.

Mine tend to happen whilst in the shower. You might find that at a time of relaxation it happens for you such as meditating or drifting off to sleep.

I wasn't thinking about anything at all, just pulling my cards, when I heard the words 'Psychic Salon'.

Oh my god! This was it!

I should start offering readings from my little room inside this salon!

So that was just what I did! It didn't take long to get bookings at all. Even though I explained I was new to reading directly for people, I was still bringing such amazing evidence and my clients soon began spreading the word.

I soon began offering a service that meant I could go out to people's homes and do readings for a group of them at a time.

I began taking bookings. I was so scared but I worked through the fear. I refused to allow it to block me from my new venture.

That very first booking was so nerve wracking for me. I got dropped off and the walk up the host's driveway felt like forever and a day. I remember ringing the doorbell as I arrived and being greeted in.

I was stood in the kitchen waiting for the host to take the lead and tell me where she wanted me, but the group just began chatting. I felt a little awkward.

Then one of the ladies said, "So when is this Psychic coming then?"

I proceeded to tell them that it was me. I was in fact the Psychic.

They were all so shocked. They hadn't met me before. They told me that I didn't look like a Psychic. That was the first time I heard that, but certainly not the last. I asked what they were expecting, not quite knowing what they were referring to.

Apparently they were expecting a much older woman, with big untamed hair. A woman who dressed 'spiritual' and probably had a cross necklace around her neck. Somebody a little more 'gothic' looking.

I was stunned. I didn't take offence, but I was so surprised that people had these expectations of what a woman with a spiritual gift should be like on the outside. Surely that wasn't a 'thing'?

The night went well and before I knew it I had another three bookings within the next twenty-four hours. This had really started something for me.

Over the coming months, my confidence grew. I was beginning to feel very comfortable speaking to people I had never met before. I was so surprised with myself as I never had confidence like this before. Until this point, I was that friend who wouldn't go to the toilet on her own on a night out, or wouldn't want to be the last one in the taxi. I was so unsure of myself after all I had previously been through that I was beginning to feel like I was finally finding myself.

Is this who I was supposed to be all along? Had I found my path, my purpose? The signs had always been there. I was meant for *'light work'*.

In between working in the salon in the day and going out to people in the evenings to give readings, I decided to sign up to a service that offered readings via text message. I was enjoying working spiritually so much, that I wanted to explore other ways. I couldn't get enough of the positive vibrations I had begun accumulating since my first spiritual connection as an adult.

How it would work was the customer would text in with what they wanted a reading about and I the reader, would reply. However, what I wasn't aware of until I signed up, was that each time a reader was very accurate (such as naming someone the reader knew who had passed away) it would be logged for the next reader to look through. Almost like a database of information about the person texting in.

But why on earth would that be necessary if the readers were genuine?

Surely they wouldn't need prior information on the person they were about to read for. Not if this work was legitimate.

Something felt insincere but I tried to ignore this instinct and instead give it a go fairly.

It was on a self-employed basis and I would probably make about fifty pence per reply I sent. It was made very clear at the beginning that the readers had to always make the reply go in to two messages. Roughly costing the customer £3 for a reply.

It was a terrible rate but I was determined to use this role as a form of practising my spiritual skills. Nothing more, nothing less.

I immediately found the owner of the company to be pretty shitty. I would finish my shift and immediately receive an email asking me why I had logged out and that I should log back in if I wanted to make decent money. He made me feel very uneasy. I felt like he was always watching me. Like he could sense what I was thinking. I didn't feel comfortable speaking with him so always kept our communication through email.

He also didn't seem to have a care about the people who were texting in. It was pretty obvious all he cared about was how fast I was replying to his customers. He wanted us, the readers, to always leave the customer wanting more. Meaning that they would then message in again. Resulting in more money for his company.

I didn't last very long doing this. I wasn't seeing a genuine light worker wanting to spread the message of spirit. I was witnessing a corrupt man who only cared to fill his pockets. I didn't have it in me to treat people this way. Especially when some of the people messaging in seemed very vulnerable and even unstable.

The moment that made me step away, was when I came

across a lady named Sue. She was thirty-five and very direct. My first interaction with her came when I received a message to ask; *"Did he notice me?"*

So I consulted spirit and passed onto her that her grandfather (who I had connected with) was implying that love wasn't going to come from the man in question, she was better off moving on from this situation.

But she would not take that for an answer. She made it very obvious she didn't want to connect with any loved ones who had passed over. She also didn't want to hear about anything other than her love life. She was fixated on this man; who she went on to name as 'Louis.'

She was insistent that Louis was in fact in love with her, he just needed to accept this. But the more and more I zoned in on this matter, the more confused I became. So I would resort to my Tarot cards, they said the same. My energy wasn't off. Neither was my connection and I didn't doubt myself at all.

There was no romance with Louis, whoever he was. He certainly didn't feel the same. There was never going to be anything romantic between them. I felt so bad for her. I didn't want to break her heart by being as blunt with her, as she was being with me. But something wasn't adding up.

She must have been spending a fortune. She would send 'REPLY' over and over in one night. There was only so many nice ways to put it for her, before I was going to upset her. So I found myself ignoring her messages.

We had around three minutes to send a response to the customer, before it would go back into the queue and another reader would end up taking on the task of reading for them.

I felt so uneasy about this one, I couldn't put my finger on it. But spirit were urging me to leave it. So I listened. It's as though they were protecting me. They didn't want me getting too involved with Sue.

A few days later, Sue arrived in my queue again. My heart sank but I decided to come to her. When I opened the message, her profile popped up too. Now I never usually read these as I wanted to go into the reading with no background information whatsoever. It felt wrong to begin a reading already knowing things about a person.

This time however, it felt necessary to see how the other readers had been getting on with Sue. So I had a look.

Whichever reader had read for her last, had commented that she had finally got to the bottom of the 'Louis' situation...

Louis, was indeed, a member of the very famous boy band 'One Direction'.

What on earth! Are you kidding me?!

It turned out, Sue had never met Louis. Not even once. They had never spoken. There certainly wasn't any romantic connection here.

She was a fan.

A *VERY* big fan of his.

Sue was clearly unstable mentally and had created an imaginary romance between the both of them. In fact, when reading through the previous messages between her and the other readers, it turned out she believed he was noticing her, through the television when she watched him from home.

I knew that I was right and this was never going to happen! This was the very reason spirit wanted me to step away from it.

I could not believe what I was reading!

It also went on to say that Sue had been blocked by the company previously, due to her messaging in that many times, that she had gotten into debt and had got into a very messy financial situation.

How had this been allowed to happen?

How was she still in the database?

I was so disturbed.

How could somebody who runs a spiritual based business be so heartless and conniving? If I wasn't already convinced he was only in it for the money, I had all the proof I needed.

So me being me, decided to investigate.

I went about messaging a few of the other readers to ask about him and his background and they had a lot to say.

He had held back their wages many times. He had private messaged some of the women with sexually motivated requests. They all agreed that he was an awful man.

So why were they still representing a company like this?

I decided there and then that I quit.

I would not be associated with a business or a man, who lacked such common decency. It was immoral and it was unacceptable. I was disgusted.

I felt like up until this point, I had been quite naïve to the fraudsters in the industry. I had continued to attend services at the church once in a while and loved to see others receive a message from spirit. But I did feel a few times that a Medium was repeating information or I felt that what they said was way too broad.

I believe it is really important to stay true to yourself when working spiritually.

Never take the 'easy route'. It's not fair to anybody to fake your abilities.

I am a massive believer in Karma and eventually you will be caught out.

There were many times where I was tested by spirit in this way. I have come across many vulnerable people desperate for a reading with me. Desperate to hear from their loved ones. But I have solid and firm boundaries. I would never read for anybody that I felt to be in a position mentally or emotionally, that could change so easily or suddenly. Potentially leading them to harm.

I still sometimes receive these lessons every now and then. It's a constant reminder as to why you have been blessed with such a gift. It's very easy to allow ego to take over. But as long as you always lead with love, spirit will continue to guide you on this journey.

On the other hand, if you're here, you're likely an empath. So you have a natural urge to want to please others and over give or over share. I for one, have had this trait for as long as I can remember. So it is even more important to create boundaries when working spiritually. You will want to give people as much of you as you can.

Back when I started reading for others, I would talk and talk and book them in even when I had blocked my time out of the diary. I found myself struggling to say no. I felt a desperate need to want to help as many people as possible. But this was wrong of me. I was taking on so much physically and spiritually. There wasn't a day of the week that I wasn't working.

There was even one time I had surgery and was back to working two days later! I soon had other mediums telling me to set strict times to stick to, so that I wasn't using up all of my energy. At the time, I dismissed it. But I soon understood what they were referring to.

You can only give so much of you before there's nothing left. I already knew too well how traumatic it is when you lose yourself.

Top Tip

When we don't set firm boundaries in our life, we often go against our own values and beliefs. This can become very draining, which will interfere with our spiritual connection. In order to connect with our higher self, we must also think about how often we commit to helping others with our spiritual gifts. If we give too much of our energy away, we have nothing left for our own tank.

When you decide to use your abilities, and strengthen your connection, commit to only doing so at certain times. Practice your abilities as much as you can at the beginning, it's normal to be motivated in this way. But be firm with your time and energy you give out to others.

In doing this, you are not only setting boundaries for you but also with spirit. Otherwise, you may be allowing spirit to communicate with you at all hours, times and ways. Being strict will also allow you to build a relationship based on trust with your Spirit Guides.

There are other ways to help you unlock your abilities and strengthen them.

The key to unlocking your gifts lies in understanding and knowing how to not only use, but also strengthen the third eye.

The third eye is a pea-sized gland called the Pineal gland. It's located between the eyes on the forehead.

It provides perception beyond eyesight. It takes us to the higher conscious, a state of enlightenment. It is the central point for your intuition. We all have one. From birth is particularly strong, which is why you hear so many stories of children seeing spirit.

Some say that when open, the third eye chakra can provide wisdom and insight, as well as deepen your spiritual connection.

While there's no scientific evidence to support these claims, many traditions and cultures emphasize the importance of the third eye chakra.

There are signs you may experience when it is beginning to open and you are beginning to connect. Such as;

Feeling comfortable in your own body

Once you begin to accept that you do have a special gift,

you become less bothered about physical appearance. You begin to feel more comfortable because you know there is so much more to you than what others can see. You are able to see through third eye vision so appearance becomes less important to you.

I used to wear make-up and did so from the very young age of around eleven years old. I always wore foundation even though I had a decent complexion. Once I really recovered my gift and recovered from my limiting beliefs, I learned to let go of that need for make-up.

I wore it for others. So, they didn't have anything to criticise when they looked at me. Now, I wear it because I want to. I stopped wearing foundation a long time ago and embrace my skin for what it is, pure.

Begin a journey of self-development and improvement

You may have already begun signing up for courses, or seeking out personal development books in order to find some sort of answers. You may start to analyse your behaviours and those around you and want to get to the root of why people are the way they are. This is a strong indication that you are wanting to make an impact. You are craving knowledge and want to release the best version of you.

Enjoying your own company and downsizing your circle

This seems to be one sign most of us experience. As soon as you begin to get serious about your development, you will naturally feel pulled to step away from the *energy vampires* in your life. These are people who live by the '3 C's' (as I like to refer to them) People who: *Complain. Criticize. Compare.*

You will find that you want to spend your time and energy around people who live with gratitude, people who focus on solutions and not problems, people who accept you. You will naturally become more consciously selective over who has access to you. With your awakening comes revelation in the form of priorities. You won't want to waste your newfound creative energy on the wrong people, and may find yourself spending more time alone. You will accept your gift and treat it as such, so don't give such a beautiful gift to those who won't appreciate it.

Becoming more aware of things going on around you

You will begin to feel like you have a sixth sense. Energy reading will increase for you, whether you choose it or not. You will walk into a room and instantly be able to judge the vibe. You will be waiting on news and sense the outcome before you have your clarification. With spiritual awareness comes deeper awareness of your senses.

Physically you may have frequent headaches and pressure build up around the ears- things such as Tinnitus are common.

What a lot of us don't understand is that as much as our limiting beliefs and life experiences can block our third eye connection, so can physical factors too. Such as:

CALCIFICATION

Calcification is the build-up of calcium phosphate crystals in various parts of the body. This process occurs because of toxins in everyday products like fluoride, artificial sweeteners, hormones, sugars.

When my Grandad Austin became poorly when I was twenty-seven with brain cancer, he began obsessively researching everything he could about how to treat it naturally. He also honed in on any typical ailments any of us in the family were experiencing. He was a man who loved to learn. He was very science based and spent the last year of his life ensuring the family had a heap of knowledge to treat themselves for any conditions we may come up against. He was a great man.

It was him who informed me about calcification. He shared with me how fluoride was so very destructive and together we looked at different studies from many scientists. We came to the conclusion that we needed to remove it from our lives. So that was how I stopped drinking tap water. I also began making my own toothpaste, although there are many fluoride-free types out there now.

Such a simple change made a huge difference, as it was between the ages of thirty until now where I feel my biggest spiritual breakthroughs have taken place. I felt healthier and more connected quite instantly. The cloudiness and blurry visions became much clearer.

What you may not realise is, your body is like your working environment. So the better you treat it, the more productivity you will get from it. Your third eye will thank you.

When I am rundown, not taking my supplements and lacking sleep, my connection is interrupted. If you can imagine it like a radio station- Spirit FM. If there is a poor signal the frequency is poor or low. It's just the same with your connection.

Make it a priority to take care of all of it; the physical, mental, emotional and spiritual as they all come together to give you the answers you seek.

In order to *recover* your connection and keep it at an aligned frequency, try to incorporate some new habits. You don't have to change everything about your life at all, I still have the odd can of Coca Cola, McDonalds and a boozy night out with friends. But I am very aware that my connection after this will be affected so I bring in some other rituals to raise my frequency. Imbalance will impact your energy massively.

Any chance I could get I was reading for people. I loved it. One of the best ways to strengthen your connection is to practice. It helps with your development but also in your trust.

You have to trust spirit and their messages in order to be a great messenger. Whether you decide to read for others for a profession or to help out loved ones from time to time. I can almost guarantee that once you unlock your gift, you won't want to keep it to yourself. You will want to share the unbelievable things you see and hear, it's hard to keep to yourself once you have built the trust within.

Once you **recover** the essence, your psyche, whether it was stolen from you or you lost it, life will become brighter. Like a beam of golden light surrounding you. Your aura amplifies. The frequency you embody will be one that is magical, paradigm shifting and awe-inspiring.

The *Spiritual Awakening* is at the core of every soul's quest for freedom and happiness.

This is an evolutionary process.

As you heal, you evolve.

As you evolve, you **recover**.

You will become more free from the chains that have held you down.

The recovery of that Magick, within the layers of who you are and what you've experienced, is a process.

A life-changing, transformational, evolutionary process.

CHAPTER 5

Re-Connect

RECONNECT- TO RE-ESTABLISH A BOND OF COMMUNICATION OR EMOTION

Your main goal in this step is to establish trust with your senses, spirit and YOU. In doing this you allow your development to flourish much quicker.

After six years, I stopped attending the spiritualist church. I felt I had outgrown it and could no longer take any further learning from it. I realised I had stayed as long as I had due to loyalty and people pleasing. I was visiting, to help others out. I was also still going, just to spend some time with my dad.

It was upon leaving the church that I came to a true place of reconnection. I had become very aware of my body and things it was telling me, as well as my psychic abilities.

I knew this because it was in my early days of attending the church that I recovered from years of hearing problems and inflammation.

From being very young I had problems with my ears. Week after week I had ear aches that were so bad, emergency doctors would be called out. I had my ears syringed regularly and the doctors said I had lots of scarring deep inside. But looking further into things, we discovered I had *Eustachian Tube Dysfunction*. This contributed to my poor hearing and the constant pain of feeling full inside my ears and head. There was often a build-up of pressure that just couldn't be relieved.

After a few times of sitting with the person I was to read for, I would sense spirit come through, when suddenly my left ear would pop. I was aware of it happening every single time, because it was something I wasn't able to do. This was why I had so much pain.

I soon realised that my ear would pop right at the time spirit would enter.

What was this all about? Why was this happening?

It was great to have this expectation as I began to feel more confident that I was developing well. But the best part was that now my ear was popping regularly, I began to find that my ear problems were becoming less frequent.

My mind was blown!

All those years of suffering, missing school, crying through the night, were over the second I re-connected with spirit.

This is something you will have happen too. A lot of women complain of some form of ailment that impacts them on a frequent basis. Often things they've suffered with for years that have gradually got worse over time. But as soon as they learn how to use their spiritual gifts, they begin to improve their overall health. This is a combination of raising the frequency of your vibrations and the changes made to strengthen your third eye.

By putting this to work, you will naturally enhance your intuition and heal your body. This comes from the power of trusting what your psyche is telling you. Your psyche will draw you to what needs healing and show you the way.

For me, it started with healing my childhood nightmare problems with my ears. But it soon impacted me on a much deeper and powerful level.

This isn't a new concept. This has been evidential for thousands of years. The women before us, the different cultures of the world have all used the force of their spiritual connection to improve their well-being.

Another example of how trusting your abilities can heal you physically is by sharing with you my long-standing journey of infertility.

For as long as I could remember, I had said I didn't want children. Throughout my entire childhood and into adulthood, I stood by this decision. It didn't stop the pressure I got from other women though. I was constantly asked when I was going to have them. Then why I didn't want them. It was awful.

Especially considering deep down, I knew I'd be a great mum.

For many years, I had a gut instinct that I would have a problem with conception. Something deep down in my womb was telling me so. I always seemed to have problems with my female organs. Ever since my first relationship, I had completely disconnected with my body. I didn't like it, I had no love for it.

So when I was twenty-six and was sat in the garden one summers day talking away with spirit in my head, I turned to James and told him that I'd changed my mind and I did want children. He smiled and said 'ok'.

But I still knew that it wasn't going to be easy. I didn't say anything to him at the time, but I had an overpowering feeling of needing to have some tests to find out once and for all. We went down that route and it turned out my gut feeling was spot on yet again. What started with blood tests, escalated to a three-and-a-half-hour surgery. I awoke to be told by my surgeon that I was a "mess down there", but that I'm healed now so I should go and try naturally for a year.

I was on a ward with women who had had surgery to take away cancer, women who had female organs removed who were smiling and cheering for me at my news.

But I heard spirit in my ear, telling me not to believe a word of what this doctor had just said. Something felt off. I wasn't smiling or cheering along.

So I turned to James and told him that I didn't trust this doctor.

"Can we please just go straight for the IVF treatment instead of trying naturally?"

He trusted me. He knew by now that my intuition always came through for me, for us.

One instance a couple of years before, I had bought him a diary for his business.

But he didn't have a business. He didn't even have plans too at the time. But I told him I knew he would before the end of the year. By that November, he had registered as a sole trader working as an electrician.

So he would always have trusted me over someone he had just met, even if they had credentials after their name.

Spirit had been right as always. The doctor in question had got it totally wrong. He had what I can only describe as a 'God complex'. He hadn't healed anything. He had attempted to, but he never should have tried to talk me out of continuing down the path of treatment.

It was not possible for me to conceive, IVF was our only option.

It took us four years to conceive. By this point we had had one cycle of IUI treatment and two rounds of IVF.

I had worked so hard at building a connection with my body. I used it daily in my readings when spirit would let me feel how they had passed over. I would also feel the ailments of the person I was reading for. I would know instantly that if I had a shooting pain in my right rib, I had somebody step through from spirit who had lung cancer. I would be aware of somebody who had a stroke when I would struggle to get my words out.

It was one of my strongest senses. The ability to feel on my own body when something was wrong.

So it was no surprise, the cycle we conceived, I *knew* I was pregnant long before taking a test. Not only that, but I also stated from the get go that I was carrying twins.

I had really connected with my *Clair sense- Claircognizance*.

When connecting with your gift, you will need to be aware of your 'Clair' senses.

CLAIRS

Your *Clairs* are the different ways you connect with spirit. They are the senses you use to distinguish whether you are in the presence of other energies. If you want to be more intuitively connected to your life, you must develop your *Clair* senses.

The most well-known one is **Clairvoyance**.

Clairvoyance is the ability *to see*.

You may see spirit, just as I did when I was seven years old. Or you may be see objects and other things. Quite often my students see images in the form of photographs. I myself, will often see words and names instead of hearing them.

Clairaudience- *To hear*.

Clairaudience is the ability to hear messages. You may hear voices, songs or strange sounds.

This was my first Clair I used when I began reading for others. I didn't realise I was already hearing so much but hadn't made the connection to it being spirit.

A few years ago now, I had gone to the sunbed with my mum and a family friend. As I stood in the sunbed, there was music playing through the speakers. A song came on that I remembered from being a kid. It was by Lutricia

McNeal titled Stranded. I was just beginning to listen when I heard a voice I recognised.

It was Graham.

Graham was the late husband of my mum's best friend Lynne and step-dad to my friend, her daughter, Stacey.

He had passed a few years before.

I listened as he told me to tell Lynne, to listen to the words of the song. Not only that, but he wanted to wish her a *Happy Anniversary*.

When I came out of the room, it must have been obvious, as I remember Stacey looking at me as though I had seen a ghost! I told all of them what had happened and Lynne was smiling. She said their anniversary was coming up in a few weeks' time! The message meant a lot to her as she was planning on moving abroad and was feeling guilty about moving on with her life. But he had said he wanted her to be happy.

It brought them all so much peace.

Clairsentience- *To sense.*

The ability to feel. You will sense somebody's emotions and feel them as if they are your own. You will also feel physically somebody else's pain, such as ailments, conditions and even on a psychic level. You may sense when something is going to happen to somebody physically, such as an accident or surgery, by feeling drawn to somewhere on your own body. This is a common sense to have amongst women who are spiritually developing.

It's often overlooked as you can confuse what you are sensing as your own pain. For example- have you ever been in the company of a friend and the whole time you're there you have an awful headache or a pain in your back? You will assume at first, that it's yours. But you didn't have any pain before arriving. Once you leave their company, the pain will begin to subside too.

Clairalience- *To smell.*

A lot of people have this ability but don't realise how beautiful it is. Have you ever randomly smelt something that instantly reminds you of a loved one that's crossed over? I have heard loads of stories of the smell of a loved one's perfume or aftershave coming into the room all by itself. It's a subtle sense but one with such magnitude.

I will often during a reading, smell alcohol strongly if I have a soul step in who would have been an alcoholic or owned a pub.

Clairgustance- *To taste.*

I don't often get to experience this sense as much as I would like to. But when I have, it's the strangest experience. One of the ways which I get to use it in a reading is when I have spirit come through and make me aware that the person I'm reading for is diabetic.

My dad is a type one diabetic and many years ago, when I used to attend the spiritualist church with my dad, he would also be working spiritually. He had told me that when he was going to become unwell with his diabetes, his breath would smell like the sweet 'Pear Drops'. He would give a reading to somebody and when he tasted that sweet, he would know what it meant. Before long, I too had picked up that same clue and it's stuck.

Claircognizance- *To know.*

The ability to just *know* things. This is an incredible sense to use and really powerful when communicating with psychic awareness. I have had this most of my life and it never loses its magick appeal.

With this *Clair sense*, I have predicted many life changing events for people.

Once, I even predicted a lottery win for somebody I actually knew! Within a month she had won one million pounds on the lottery!

Your *Clair senses* play a pivotal part in your journey so the sooner you get to recognising them the better. The *Clair senses* are like muscles; they are always there. They will never disappear but there will be times when you become familiar with one in particular, only to find a new one replaces it unexpectedly. You can practise strengthening them right away. I have some practical tasks for you in the final chapter of this book.

When we got our very first positive pregnancy test, we were in Tenerife on holiday. We had made it our mission to get away during that time as our last cycle, which failed, was heart-breaking. Not only that, but I had lost my darling Loulou, my fifteen-year-old Chihuahua afterwards. She was our baby and nothing compared to the love I had for her. We always knew each other inside out and even shared the same life-path number of thirty-three.

I had told James after our first cycle failed that we wouldn't have a baby until Loulou was no longer with us. I could feel it so strongly. I knew I couldn't share my heart with a baby whilst she had my undivided attention.

Out of nowhere, on Boxing Day 2016, Loulou became unwell. She was always so spritely and always bounding around. After rushing her to the emergency vet, we were told we had a few months left with Loulou as she was dying from heart failure. But Loulou passed away in my arms on the 8th January 2017 just a few days later. We had our positive result eight weeks later on the 8th March.

In between those eight weeks, I noticed the number thirty-three everywhere. From number plates on cars, to receiving letters in the post addressed to number thirty-three, when we were in fact number forty-three! It was too often to be a coincidence. I knew Loulou was behind it due to our significance to the number thirty-three. She sent me so many signs during that time and even continues to even today.

When we arrived in Tenerife it began to happen again. I made a point of showing James every single time. He soon acknowledged there was something spiritual about this all. He acknowledged this was no coincidence.

So when we got that positive result, I wasn't surprised.

After four years, we finally had our news. We went for our early scan with the treatment centre and laying on that bed, I was waiting for the nurse to say, "Wow it's twins". But she didn't.

Instead, she turned the screen to face us and said, "Here's your healthy baby.".

My face must have been a picture! I was adamant that it was twins. I must have looked so disappointed, but I was genuinely surprised. She clearly picked up on my expression and asked what was wrong. I told her I was so sure it was twins, I was happy, just shocked.

This spurred her into taking another look around and low and behold her face became a sight!

"Oh my goodness, there is two! The other one is here, just behind the first one! It was hiding!"

Then she said they were identical twins! They were sharing one placenta; this is how she knew.

I found that moment hysterical. I just knew I was right. I could sense it all along. I had nothing to compare it to as I'd never been pregnant before.

I didn't need to be sat in meditation or practice setting an intention to be able to connect with my senses. After all of my previous effort and commitment over the years, I was so in tune with it. It guided me. I was led by it. I trusted it entirely. My gift was second nature to me now. I never second guessed my first feeling or thought.

That is where these *Five Steps* will get you. Once you create new habits out of these steps, you will have such a strong connection that you don't even have to think about it. Your answers will come from within. You won't question it.

With that in mind, it is still good practise to try to set some boundaries from the get go. This allows you to come from a place of intent. This will save you a lot of time stepping into one energy to the next and becoming drained.

Remember, to have a great connection, maintain a happy work environment.

I like to use three techniques to enable myself to go from 'open' to 'closed' when working with spirit for others benefit.

So if I am getting ready to host a show, or a bunch of readings are coming up, I will first do these three things to prep me, so that I do my best job.

NUMBER ONE- GROUNDING

Grounding and rooting yourself to the physical earth before connecting with spirit is essential. It keeps you rooted in yourself, your values and your ethics, no matter who or what you connect to in spirit.

You may have heard of some women who visualize themselves connecting to the earth, with roots coming from their feet and into the ground.

But that's never really worked for me, if anything it freaks me out a little. I'm not comfortable and much prefer to stay true to that. So as you can see, if it doesn't feel right, if it doesn't feel like 'you', then don't do it. Find your own way.

When I talk about 'grounding' I much prefer it in the physical realm. So I will spend a few hours out in nature so that I can feel connected to Earth. The planet where I have spent many lifetimes and where my ancestral lineage comes from. I will walk in the woods, with all the trees and imagine my ancestors walking with me. I try to do this as much as possible, especially when I feel like I'm surrounded by a concrete jungle. Sometimes when the walls are closing in and I feel very *human*, I decide to get out to nature, to bring me back to where I *really* come from.

I take in the air around me and allow the sun to gaze down and charge my third eye ready for my event. It helps me to feel aligned. If I don't have time due to being a typical mum of young children, then I will spend time out in the garden amongst nature. Listening to the birds singing, the buzzing of the bees and the feel of the cool grass beneath my feet is quite often all I need anyway.

It's important to pay attention to that point. You could be busy being a mum and not always able to spend lots of time doing the things that are fulfilling to the soul. You might be caring for a family member, or working all hours of the day. So it's only fair to give yourself understanding of this. You can still ground yourself, but when you are able. Don't ever allow this to put you under pressure. Remember- there are no rules here.

NUMBER TWO- CLEAR OUT

Clearing out any non-essential emotions and thoughts prior to connecting with spirit with is key to clear communication. Releasing past, present or future worries and anxieties will allow you to be fully in the present moment.

The reason I believe this is so relevant with connection is because if you attempt to open up your third eye right after a huge argument with your partner, your connection will suffer. This is because you are naturally distracted and your head, heart and body will be out of whack. Your energy will be off as it's coming from a place that isn't particularly calm.

It's only happened on a few occasions, but I've had bookings that I've had to cancel or rearrange due to a problem arising that's meant I just can't get into it. My connection has suffered.

For example, before Nanny Carla passed away a few years ago, she was poorly in hospital for a whole month before. I went to see her every single day. Then the day came that we were all dreading. I was on my way to the hospital that evening when I got a phone call on the way to say she had just passed away. I was devastated. I had made a point that I was to be the one called as I just HAD to be there with her so that she wasn't alone. But it wasn't meant to be.

During this time, there were days I was ok to continue with my work commitments that night, but others I just couldn't.

The problem was, I was so busy. I had so many bookings. Not only that, but we were also going through another round of IVF. The boys were almost two and we were desperate for one more addition to the family. The night before Nanny passed away, I whispered in her ear, that the very next morning we would be having our embryos transferred and I would be pregnant. Nobody knew, it was our secret.

That next morning, I went to the clinic for my transfer and by that same evening, Nanny had passed away.

With all this going on, I did struggle connecting with spirit.

How am I expected to bring forward this person's loved one, when I was wishing to hear from mine? I felt jealous.

I didn't have the right energy to bring forward a connection for somebody else. So there were a few cancellations around this time.

I was out of alignment.

I fully listened to what my heart needed at this time. But also my body. I had to put 'me' first.

One of the ways you can 'clear out' is to take three deep breaths whilst imagining all the emotions and thoughts within you, being released into the air around you like smoke, and then settling back down around your feet, to the ground. With every breath out, release them so you are no longer holding onto them.

Then you can visualise a golden white light surrounding you, like a bubble. This is a bubble of protection. This white light is your protection from any negative energies which may try to connect to you.

When giving readings to others, you may also want to

ensure you protect them too by visualising them surrounded in white light also.

When I talk about 'negative energies' this means a variety of things.

One being, protecting yourself from anything negative that's been projected onto you, such as friends or family's bad moods that day. Or something I may have seen on television or in the news.

I've heard stories about demons and bad spirits, but to this day, it's not something I've come across. Regardless, it's not something I would want to leave to chance, which is why I do take protection seriously for myself and my clients.

You should too. Protection comes in different forms. As long as the intention is there to keep protected, you will be fine.

And lastly…

NUMBER THREE- PRAYER OF INTENTION

The final step is setting a goal for the outcome of your connection with Spirit. This is often called an intention (a determination to act a certain way) or a prayer (an earnest hope or wish, a request for help).

Some mediums say a prayer for intention, some say a prayer for protection.

I prefer to use a mix of the both. I say my prayer of intention every time I am ready to open up connect with spirit. This enables me to have some form of routine so I can get the answers I am needing.

These three habits I created don't necessarily strengthen my connection, except for grounding, but they do enable me to be 'ready' to connect at a given time.

You may wonder then why when you watch a TV show or something that the medium seems to be communicating with spirit all the time, without warning and without being in control. I used to wonder the same. It is possible to constantly receive messages from spirit. But with that comes the exhaustion. If you don't set something in place, you will get to a point of being drained by it all.

Do you already connect with spirit? If so, start incorporating these three steps to ensure you don't leave yourself drained of your energy.

By practising these three steps, it will help to give you some control with spirit. Have these things in place to keep the control and to feel safe. Spirit cannot be allowed to take over, otherwise you will be bombarded with messages everywhere you go. The overwhelm you will feel, will be physically off putting as well as leaving you feeling anxious. Possibly wanting to stop for a while. So it is worth you committing to *something*.

CHAPTER 6

Revive

REVIVE- TO RESTORE TO LIFE OR
CONSCIOUSNESS

B y building a connection with your spirit
guides, your ancestors and the women
before you, you allow healing and restoration to flow through you. This then allows peace
and joy in abundance as you feel them come back
to life through your acceptance of your gift.

PART ONE - SPIRIT GUIDES

I was doing really well professionally. I was finding my feet
with raising twin toddlers whilst taking care of the household and running my businesses. We had bought our
dream house when the boys were a few months old and
although it was the most stressful time due to them being
born prematurely, we had everything we needed.

In fact, the very house we had bought, was the same as the

house I had drawn five years previously on a piece of paper, when I first started to embrace the *Law of Attraction*. It had the garage conversion, I'd even drawn two little dogs into the picture which just so happened to fit too. We already had Coco and six months after Loulou had passed away, we found our Lola. It had all come together for us.

But even though I was happy, I was still wanting more.

That little voice would creep in at times when I wanted more, but not this time. I realised then that I had conquered my inner voice that belonged to generations before me.

You know the narrative of:

   More? You have enough."

   You should be grateful. You've got an amazing family and doing well."

But why does, "well" mean enough? It doesn't. Why are limits placed upon our wants, needs and dreams?

I've never heard anybody say this to James. Or any male close to me in fact. The men are encouraged to strive for more. We have been conditioned to be grateful for what we have and not expect too much.

It's ok to want more. It's incredible to be ambitious and determined. Once you begin working spiritually, you will connect with your purpose and once that happens, there will be nothing holding you back.

Imagine this- you come to a point in your life where everything is great. You have everything you always wanted. So what next? What comes after you have what you want?

To me, it only makes sense to move the goalpost and begin learning again. Start giving your soul some real TLC by allowing it to evolve and revive. When we dedicate time to our spiritual gifts, it allows us to grow on a soul-level. If we can go deeper and deeper, we can uncover so many revelations about us and where we come from.

I know how hard it is to give yourself such valuable time. You're probably thinking "it's not as easy as that". I know, I get it. I've often thought, if only I had been able to dig deeper *before* my children came along. But that's the thing, we take time for granted.

I've been able to grow and progress further since becoming a mother. Before my children, I lacked direction. But since having them, they gave me bigger reasons to commit. I can't be the best mother to them, if I can't give back time to myself.

It's just another of society's patriarchal expectations of women. To have to sacrifice, sacrifice, sacrifice! It doesn't have to be this way.

You really can have it all.

I felt it was time for me to connect with my *Spirit Guides* to see if there was something more that I was needing to know…

Spirit Guides are not physical beings and are not bound by the laws of the universe, they come in different forms and have unique purposes. The common goal is to help guide you back into alignment with your soul contract. They are always with you whether you know it or not. We tend to have a team of guides up there. Your spiritual team will never lead you down a wrong path. They will help you to discover what you are here to do. You can call on your spirit guides whenever you feel.

I sat in the garden listening to some soft calming music and went into a meditative state. It soon became apparent I wasn't alone in this place of peace I like to go to in my mind's eye.

I discovered I had a new guide.

He came in and was of Native Indian decent. He was a tall man with long white hair, with flicks of dark grey. He smiled and sat on the floor and crossed his legs. He had a circle of stones around him. He picked two of them and began hitting them together, making them spark. I felt pulled to sit too, so followed his lead.

With a very deep voice he said the word, "Oto".

I hadn't heard that word before, so knew I would remember it to bring back once I came out of the meditation. I asked him what I need to know. He said "You are here to be a Doctor. You are here to save people from themselves."

I further asked him if there was anything else I needed to hear and he told me to be thankful for the lessons I am receiving.

When I came out of the meditation, I instinctively wanted to research the word "Oto" as the curiosity would eat away at me otherwise.

I was stunned with what I was met with:

'Oto' was a tribe that lived as a semi-nomadic people on the Central Plains along the bank of the Missouri River in Nebraska, Kansas, Iowa and Missouri. The Oto-Missouria hunted bison, gathered plants, and grew corn, beans, pumpkins, and squash. They believed in Wakanda, a universal spirit.

I was so intrigued as to what he meant when he said I would be a Doctor. I knew it couldn't mean a 'doctor' in the typical western way as I am somebody who turns to Mother Earth to heal before reaching out for 'medication'. So it must mean something connected to alternative healing.

I didn't realise it at the time, but I was already healing people. I had been most of my life. But surely my mediumship and psychic work didn't amount to the same gravity of healing a Doctor does?

Maybe my guide meant I would heal a certain problem, or group of people?

What I teach my students, is that meeting your Spirit Guide is vital in spiritual connection. Your Spirit Guide will take you into your journey, you will never feel alone and you will feel safe. Which is what you need from day one.

You want to meet your Spirit Guide as soon as you can, so make some time for this.

I do want to point out that not everybody will have it happen immediately, so don't apply pressure. When you are ready to meet your guide, they will appear.

In the last chapter of this book, you will find a meditation I have created specifically for you to use, to help you connect with your Spirit Guide.

Another way a Spirit Guide can help you is by being the vessel between you and spirit. For example, people will naturally assume I am speaking directly with their loved one, but in reality, often it is my guide translating. They will often appear first, to bring the soul through. If I connect with a spirit who spoke a foreign language I wouldn't understand, my guide will be the translator in between us.

It is important to take the time to get to know your Spirit Guide as this means you are going to build trust. Your guides will be the ones who take you to your 'sacred place' where you will often go to reflect in meditation. Your guides will keep you safe and help you along your soul contract. You have to access your Clair senses to take in the messages they provide. To truly listen is important.

Once you begin to feel comfortable with your guide, in will enter a new one. This just happens, with no warning. You may sense leading up to it, that your senses are changing, that you are connecting differently with your gifts. But once a new guide comes in, also work on building a connection. Each guide will teach you something different, they will have their own unique ways. They may also send you a particular sign when it is them, that is coming through. This way you begin to recognise who is with you.

I began to feel a shift in the way I was working. I found myself having an urge to research, to learn. This desire is often a reflection of what spirit are trying to direct you towards. The next part of your path. I was beginning to feel a huge connection to my ancestry and my womb since Nanny Carla passed away.

A few weeks after Nanny passed, we also lost the baby. It was a devastating miscarriage as I had also placed my own expectation on it to be something that would help everybody through their grieving of Nanny. But it wasn't meant to be.

A while passed and I was thinking more and more about wanting another baby. James and I had already discussed going again, but IVF puts a huge strain on the body physically and I was so busy with work commitments, it would have to time in with a point where I would have less going on. I knew though that something was holding me back, there was something I needed to heal within before I could have what I truly wanted.

Spirit told me to try Reiki. I'd never had it before, like most holistic treatments.

Like I said, you can be spiritual without having tried everything.

It was something I often thought about having, but never felt I had a reason to.

But now I did.

With absolute synchronicity, at the same time it came to mind, my friend Sophia began advertising her Reiki business as she was newly qualified.

So I reached out and she was thrilled for me to try. I didn't know what I was expecting. I don't think I had any expectations to be honest, but I'm open minded and was willing to seek answers for my soul.

So the night came where she rang me to explain what would happen. She would send out the healing from where she was, whilst I would listen to some music she sent over and fully relax in the moment.

This should be easy then, I thought. Still not knowing what would happen.

What must have only been a few seconds turned into a life changing moment.

I remember being in a field and overlooking what looked like a meadow. When I walked into it, I saw a white horse galloping. But as I got closer, I saw a little boy sat on the horse. I instinctively knew he was mine. He looked just like my little boy Ace, but this boy's hair was darker. But the same face more or less. Judging his size, he would be about the age my baby would have been now, had we not have had our loss.

Suddenly I was very aware of tears rolling down my face and with every breath out I was feeling more relieved.

It was as though I was releasing something I had held onto in that moment.

It may sound unbelievable to some, but in that moment I was healing from within. Not only from my miscarriage, but also from the physical changes I had been experiencing since then. I thought my body had changed since having my boys, but in actual fact, things had got worse since my miscarriage.

My cycles were much heavier than before. The cramps I

had were much more intense. Doctors repeated that it was normal after having a child.

I never connected the dots until this moment. The grief I still held was impacting me on a physical level, my body had been telling me so. Maybe my cycle issues were down to trauma and not a physical problem that needed resolving with surgeries and medications.

I just remember I felt that physically, something had been repaired.

I soon saw somebody else appear. It was Nanny Carla. She helped the boy off the horse and held his hand. She smiled at me and they turned and began to walk away. All of them dressed in white, along with the white horse, held the significant look of angels. It was so very real and I awoke to the music being stopped. I checked the time and it had been only twenty minutes of me laying on my bed. I wiped the tears off my face and spent a few minutes studying what had just happened. I had to figure out what was happening, what was I to remember from all of this.

I knew instinctively that little boy was my baby growing in spirit. I also knew that Nanny Carla felt a special connection to him, as she was the first person to know he was being created back on that day before she passed over. I was beginning to realise that my body's conception issues may be healed naturally by healing my spiritual connection to my body.

Deal with the pain so the emotion doesn't stay trapped in your body. Emotion is energy trapped 'in motion'. Allow your soul to be free.

I had never been able to conceive, this stemmed from my abusive relationship. Perhaps the way I felt about my body, the traumas it had faced, were limiting its potential.

I suddenly felt empowered that my spiritual gifts were going to bring my body back to life. Almost like a physical renewal. It was necessary if we were to head back into IVF.

PART TWO - FEMININE POWER

Have you felt a disconnect from your body?

Have previous experiences or limiting beliefs created a perception of dislike or shame around your body?

Have you ever considered that the way women's bodies are perceived by society could potentially have caused the disconnect?

HEAR ME OUT.

How do you view your menstrual cycle? A burden? An inconvenience?

How many times growing up were you embarrassed about being on your bleed? Worried that a boy would know and point it out to your peers? Did you used to send a parent to the shop to buy your sanitary towels or tampons?

Does the fact that I use the word 'bleed' make you uncomfortable?

In some cultures, back in the 18th century, rituals would be performed for a menstruating girl. Her very first period would be celebrated by the tribe, and they would hold a year-long feast for the whole community. Purely to celebrate the girls transition.

Imagine- a year-long consideration of the power of her womanhood.

In one said tribe today, menstruating girls are secluded, but not out of shame, instead to allow them time to rest without chores and give her space to work on her personal and spiritual growth.

Indigenous people believe a girls first period to be a time when women are at their most spiritually powerful and is often a time, they will have visions.

Compare that to your society.

Are YOU celebrated for being a woman and having the most natural bodily function?

It's ok to sell what's between a woman's legs, more than it's ok to speak about the inner workings.

The way we experience our first menstruation will leave an imprint on us forever. Unless we actively seek to reprogramme and transform the way we view our bodies. We will otherwise keep playing out the same ancestral wounding patterns that have been present in our lineage for many years.

I spent some time working on treating my body with love and not dreading the 'womanly' processes it goes through. I instead began to embrace everything with love and gratitude. I had never felt closer to my body. I began to view it from a perspective of admiration and appreciate all it had done for me. It had survived operations, always recovered so well from medications and treatments. It had bounced back time and time again and I was determined that with some proper investment into taking care of it, it would **revive** and go on to create what I needed from it.

I decided to go into my past lives to see if something would come up that would maybe help me understand what I needed to do before I could have another baby. That's something I've learned through my gifts. To lean into the learnings, instead of just the trauma. Take it all in and feel through it.

This year, we went again for another round of treatment. I had put a lot of relationship work in with my body. I loved her. I respected her. I felt more in tune with my feminine energies. I truly felt I had put the work in so the time was now to try again for our third baby.

I knew I was pregnant before doing a test as usual.

I knew within a couple of days of the embryo transfer. I always have.

But something was niggling away at me. I knew the baby was ok as I could sense that, but I just couldn't relax. I felt that something was going to go wrong.

It isn't like me to expect the worst, I'm actually the opposite to that. I felt that we had been through so much during this journey that I looked at the things that hadn't happened to us. The only thing that stood out to me, that hadn't happened previously, was an ectopic pregnancy. We had experienced everything else, from miscarriage, twins, C-section, premature births.

So I messaged the fertility clinic to explain my feelings, but of course they told me not to worry. That everything must be fine as I had no signs of having an ectopic pregnancy.

The day of our scan arrived and I was preparing myself to hear what I already knew. As I laid there, waiting for the nurse to smile, she turned the screen towards us. What should have been the womb with an obvious baby, was an empty space.

But I KNEW I was pregnant.

She said the words "I'm so sorry".

I finished the rest of her sentence. "It's ectopic isn't it?"

"Yes, I'm so sorry your baby is alive and has a healthy heartbeat."

Never did I imagine hearing those words used negatively, apologetically.

I was devastated I was right. As was James.

We cried and cried until she said she had to go and ring an ambulance as I would need surgery to remove the baby immediately. This was an emergency. I was at risk of my fallopian tube rupturing.

Now you're probably wondering why being so psychic and in tune with my gift is such a good thing at times such as this. But my point is this, since day one of my infertility journey I was made aware that my fallopian tubes were completely blocked. They were the reason I was infertile. Many procedures and surgery had been performed.

So if they were so blocked, how on earth was that little embryo able to move its way up there and implant securely?

The nurses seemed stunned that my right tube was now clear. It was no longer blocked. Although I resorted to having my tubes removed, ultimately just knowing that when I had that Reiki and felt I was healing internally, I was right all along.

My tubes were still completely blocked after the miscarriage, so it had been between then and now, that the right one had healed. The doctors at the hospital were amazed at how the little one was still going strong as they believed from a medical point of view, that it shouldn't still be growing, considering the tube was so dramatically stretched and filled with toxic fluid.

I had been told for years my tubes were damaged and an egg could never get through them. But I refused to have them removed for all those years as I believed one day, they might heal.

I believe in miracles.

Through healing through my previous traumas, the power of spiritual connection had revived my body. My body had healed naturally and been brought back to its original state.

I couldn't believe it!

Spirit have already made me aware that I am free now from needing to heal physically. I can now move forward with the realisation that our spiritual connection goes beyond what science can accomplish.

A huge part in our limitations as women, is that we aren't connected enough to our ancestry and our past lives. It's my belief and knowledge that without reconnecting with our lineage, we can continue to be burdened by previous generations traumas.

We often hold fear and shame around our own body wisdom due to the memories of pain and punishment.

This includes memories on a cellular level. Even if we don't remember why we are afraid, our cells do.

Women in our ancestral line were brutally punished for sharing their wisdom.

The '*Witch Wound*' is the trauma connected with the women, our ancestors before us, who weren't able to be them true selves, in fear or reprimand such as punishment by execution. It's no wonder we find it so hard to embrace our gifts, when for many years we have been punished for doing so.

Women were murdered for healing their communities. Wise women who knew how to heal naturally. You would imagine when the first execution took place, as a woman, you would have been very afraid.

I most certainly would have been sentenced to death for being accused of being a 'witch'. I think you will feel the same.

This is just a few reasons you may have:

You have a group of female friends- If you were viewed to be a group of women congregating, without a man, you were considered a 'coven' up to no good.

You are financially independent- If you were a woman who had her own money, with no help from a man, you would be isolated before being arrested and likely murdered.

You are a healer- You make your own ointments or prefer to turn to nature for healing. This would be completely unacceptable and you would have expected to be hunted down for this.

You dream about the man you will marry- Do your dreams ever come true, or do you work on manifesting things into reality? Forget about that Happy Ever After if you dared to share that with somebody!

You are struggling to conceive- Not only do you have the torment and heartache of not being able to hold a baby in your arms, you would also risk being brutally murdered, as your infertility was considered a punishment from God.

Can you imagine? For the women who came before us, they weren't able to live as they wanted to. They couldn't explore the depths of their spiritual gifts. They couldn't even scratch the surface. To think if you were alive in these times and had a beautiful dream visitation from a loved one, you couldn't possibly repeat it to anybody else. Everything had to remain hidden.

They were unlikely to live another day if they were honest about who they were deep down. The unfortunate reality is that *still* today there is this history of our spiritual abilities being something that is bad, or wrong.

To think it was that hard to accept spiritual women for who they were and the gifts they had, that society would rather remove them and make an example to other women, to not dare step out of their box. Fear was created to instil order for women.

Men didn't want women to be the more powerful.

Today, as women, we still hold onto this generational trauma. The *'witch wound'* is **very** real.

How do we heal the generational trauma? By accepting our own spiritual gifts and using them. By not being afraid of what others may think. By breaking through these barriers of the hundreds of years before us. By allowing and showing other women how to step into their power. When one of us takes the step forward, it allows other women to follow. We show all the others how magical it is to live in *Spiritual Authenticity*.

Your ancestors weren't able to be spiritually authentic in fear of death. You hold so much more freedom in your hands. Take advantage of this time that you are living in.

It is important that you enter this work for YOU first. For your body, your story. You will build the capacity to within to hold space for the bigger stories as they rise.

At some point, you're going to have to start living. You cannot hide from your gift forever. Once you move through the fear of owning who you are, there is a familiarity that will resurface.

You can choose to stay as you are, but you would soon

begin experiencing the physical signs of a constant reminder that you are supressing your connection.

Why would you want to waste another moment, when you could be experiencing the same incredible magick?

If you can let go of the reigns, spirit will take care of the rest for you. Who knows how impactful your transformation will be. The only way to find out is to go out into this world, this moment and see where your soul guides you.

I share my experiences as an example of where you can begin and where you can end up. I am very open with the world as I refuse to be kept silent any longer. I speak openly about my infertility, my heartaches and my traumas because I know another woman will feel less alone when she goes through it. I share my teachings because I know the world needs more of us women. Women with such tremendous, healing gifts. The world needs more of me. The world needs more of YOU. This is how I get to play my part to keep Mother Earth moving.

Is your body talking? Are you ready to listen?

Are you ready to return to the very wisdom inside of you?

CHAPTER 7

Rise

RISE - MOVE FROM A LOWER POSITION TO A
HIGHER ONE

By this point, you should be feeling very connected to your body, soul and heart. This is where you pay attention to the clues to reveal your soul's purpose. Let your spiritual connection unravel what you are here to do.

Even though my journey had been a difficult and somewhat emotionally draining one at times, my mind set had shifted and I felt very different to others around me. I seemed to always be coming from a place of gratitude and appreciation. Some would say I really enjoyed life. But I found that those closest to me didn't quite seem in the same place I was.

I still seemed to be met with conversations with a sprinkling of pity, or anxiety within.

I struggled to understand why there was so many people

without any ambition or drive. There was a total lack of passion in them. Now I'm an all or nothing type of woman. I don't do things half-heartedly.

A good majority of the world seemed lost.

It was then, when I put the pieces together. For, those who seemed to be lost, had a total lack of direction. No purpose.

But why?

Well from what I began to see was that, most of the women especially, who reached out to me, had found themselves living a life they just didn't set out to have.

Some had accidentally fallen pregnant and for this reason, had to leave a very good job. Some had planned children but then found themselves at the brunt of other's opinions on how she should raise her children. Usually resulting in her own dreams fading away in the distance. Others had gone through trauma that had impacted their confidence, meaning they just couldn't bring themselves to go for what they wanted.

There were just so many reasons. But what I knew would help them, was to connect with their spiritual core. By doing so, it would open up their mind to a whole new world of opportunities and blessings. A life created in the mind and moulded into their reality.

Just like I had.

If you have got to this point in your life, not being sure of what you want, then it is likely you aren't living in purpose.

To live in purpose means doing what truly matters to you in alignment with your values and beliefs. A sense of purpose means dedicating yourself to a cause beyond yourself. It's a goal that fuels your motivation in life, giving your life meaning and direction, inspiring you to make a significant contribution to the world.

Do you ever feel lost in life?

Or are you bored to death by a soul-destroying repetitive job requiring little to no creativity?

Have you chosen to live a life that you didn't actually want? Maybe to please others, such as parents?

It can be soul destroying to come to a point where you look back and question how you ended up there. Wondering why you didn't embrace your gift, or talents. Forever questioning why, you didn't follow your dreams.

Yet, there are people who willingly or unwillingly live their lives based on society's dictates and preferences. I'm talking about people who are constantly living outside their purpose and are unhappy about it. While sadness is an emotion that is as common as happiness, a constant state of sadness, will cause you to slip into a pattern of automatic negative thoughts which can be more difficult to get out of. Those without purpose tend to live a life of anxiety, always worrying about what might happen next, as they aren't planning it.

It's not a great place to be.

I have been there too. But I decided to do something about it. At the end of the day, do you want to live a life with regrets?

As with everything in spirituality, you must take action to get the results you want. But you must first understand how you got here in order to take back your purpose.

Ideally you want to be in a position where you are happy right where you are. Not focused on the past, or busy worrying about what the future holds. Just right here, in the present moment.

It's being in the present moment that creates awareness.

Try staying in a mental state of trust throughout the day when you're shopping, showering, doing laundry and cooking. Try staying in a state of trust when you're with friends and family and at work.

Moving into trust allows you to stay in a high vibrational frequency so you can attract better things to you. It allows you to move out of fear or frustration because of unmet expectations. It helps you be happier and more abundant. Spirit is on your side to help you with this. You have a whole spiritual network up there that are willing to help you every step of the way.

Top Tip

Try relaxing your entire body and expanding the energy around your third eye far to the sides forward and backward. Notice what you feel? How does this relate to the direction you've been pointing your life? Do you feel guided to change anything? Do you feel guided to change an attitude towards a situation? Often, we will not be able to trust spirit easily when we are constantly around other people. This is because we are influenced by their thoughts and may not be able to hear or have the space to hear our spirit guides.

By plugging into the present moment awareness, you may find yourself being triggered on occasion and brought back to a time from the past. Allow yourself to feel through it, then check in and say, "I accept". This will help you become aware.

Give yourself that power to be able to say, "I control what I do".

You have given away your power for too long. To family, society and even your ancestors. You have to take it back and break generational cycles. You even give your power away to people you don't know or like. When you choose not to wear that dress in case somebody has something negative to say about it. Or when you watch the news and it leaves you feeling sad and low.

By breaking the chains, you can live in the energy of courage and not fear. This is a huge step in accepting your spiritual awareness and using it to create a life you could only dream of.

Becoming the best version of yourself is the key to finding your souls purpose. It's the key to your success in business, marriage, friendships. All of this will only be as good as you are.

So you need to find who you are. You have to choose your identity. Not an identity created by other's perceptions. You have to detach. Detachment is not that you own nothing, but that nothing owns you.

You won't know what you need in life, what you want in life, until you know who you are. Your purpose will grow and evolve, just as you do.

I talk a lot about how you need to create a new identity to have a life in alignment. There are three things I focus on firstly:

Head- for vision. Your perception, what you want

Heart- awareness- Being able to understand and trust your intuition

Hand- What you give back. Your service to the world.

Without using all three of these things right here, we lose something. We sacrifice. We are unfulfilled.

If you spend some time, to think seriously about what you want from this life, you can then use your gifts for the next steps. You have to decide first WHO you are and WHAT you want.

I remember those first few years in business, really hiding my gift from people. Whenever I had to fill out a form, I wouldn't write my true occupation in the box, I would write 'self-employed' instead. I felt a little embarrassed writing the truth.

I was living in a box, one that kept me hiding from my truth. It certainly hinders your spiritual connection when you aren't coming from a place of honesty. You must fully embrace who you are and your purpose. Even when that's difficult. Even if others don't agree.

Over two years ago, the world came to a complete standstill. We all felt the pause. We were suddenly in a position where we had no control over our lives, or so it seemed. We couldn't just go out to work as normal, or visit friends at the pub. Everything changed.

We were suddenly living in a state of fear. We were living right in the middle of historical times. None of us had experienced anything like it.

For some people, they were to abide by everything they were instructed to do. They had trust in the government and were very afraid of not only the deadly disease but also the repercussions of not doing as they were told.

Others chose to keep life as normal as possible.

Me included.

I had two two-year-olds to keep occupied. As well as running a business and wouldn't receive any financial help. We couldn't just stop. There was no way I would allow disruption that we were being imposed with to affect my children's well-being. They were my number one priority.

As we stepped into this new dystopian way of life, something wasn't adding up.

From the very beginning, things felt off to me and I expressed it.

As we didn't really have anywhere to go, the world turned to social media to release its emotions and thoughts. Wherever you looked, there was talk of what was happening around the world. We were trapped, our freedom was being removed from us bit by bit. All the while I couldn't shake the feeling that we weren't really seeing things for what they were. That we were instead, being kept from the truth.

I had always been the kind of person to keep my opinions to myself. Unless, it was something I would feel extremely passionate about.

So when my intuition was guiding me to explore a whole rabbit hole of information, I knew I shouldn't keep quiet on what I was discovering. So I too, began to share my views.

This wasn't always received positively. I knew that could happen. But I refused to be silent. I felt too strongly, that as a collective, we needed to push through the fear and refuse to become consumed by it.

I had always believed in the power of manifestation, and this was just the same. The more we embraced the feeling of fear, the more we would have to be fearful about. I wanted so badly for others to step into their power and be in control of their own actions and evaluate their own situation, safety and concerns.

I wanted to protect everybody by empowering them to choose for themselves. Some didn't like it as I say and I would notice weekly, that my friends list was shrinking. I was being unfollowed and received some messages from people telling me how I should be behaving.

How I should take responsibility for others by not sharing my views.

How ironic!

But I didn't allow my ego to take over. I remained focused on my mission to continue living as normal as possible. I had never craved my freedom as much as I did now. I hated seeing so much heartache caused by this theft of our rights and freedoms. Some feared a virus. But I didn't. I feared our lives never getting back to what they were. I could already visualize the destruction that would be created. The financial crisis, the closures of small businesses. The traumatic memories people would be left with, not being able to say goodbye to their dying loved ones.

The damage was going to be catastrophic.

Spirit had communicated a lot with me during these first few months. I was receiving many messages of reassurance that I was accurate with my feelings. I was very aware six weeks before it hit the headlines, that something big was coming and it would create a negative impact. But I was also told not to be afraid, I would be ok.

All would be.

When you make decisions based on your sovereignty and intuition, you literally do not give a fuck if people agree with you or not. You certainly don't need anybody's permission or approval to stand in your own choices.

You won't see the synchronicity or the miracles if you're consumed with fear or frustration of non-acceptance. It wasn't easy at first when I began to be honest about how I felt. The majority of the human race were expressing opposing views. I didn't belittle them or throw insults. For me, it was a quantum shift in my authenticity. I was finally being me; I wasn't going to hold back to please others. Or to keep them in their comfort zone. That wasn't my responsibility.

My responsibility lied with what mattered most to me- my family and my truth. I owed it to myself to acknowledge how I felt. Instead of pushing it to the side and allowing bigger voices to overpower me.

My intentions were pure and my soul felt free. This was real freedom. I was taking back what I had lost all those years before. I felt empowered and stronger than ever.

One of my proudest moments of my life was when my husband, sister in law Christa and my boys went to the march in London. We walked the streets of Westminster, chanting amongst one million other sovereign beings. It was the most electric, incredible day. The energy was divine. One million strangers came together with the same purpose. To share love and freedom in order to create unity. Our energy was booming after that experience for days. We refused to acknowledge the news and the media and continued to live as we chose.

Some may still not agree on my views, but I know for certain a lot who questioned me, went on to change their minds. They told me so. I lived how I felt was right for my family. I had to teach my boys that they were sovereign beings and they need to choose their own paths. I shall raise powerful, kind and compassionate leaders. What the world needs more of.

I haven't always been a 'Fuck the System' person, but the last few years have awakened so much inside of me. Since Grandad Austin passed away. He taught us so much, he left a legacy. I've learned to question EVERYTHING! We live behind a smoke screen, which is why it is so important that we connect with our third eye power. There has to be a reason women were executed all those years ago for having this connection. I truly believe the elites, the richest white men in power want us to be simple beings. Our third eye connection makes us powerful, complex, smart.

There's been many wars on women. Women have had to fight for so much in this world. We've also overcome so much. Your power lies within you. You just have to unlock it to bring it to life.

This isn't a dig at men. Men too have been conditioned to be a certain way. Men have always come above women for thousands of years. It would be extremely difficult to re-programme so many years of colonization. There isn't equality anywhere in the world. Wars on women, wars on people of colour, wars on different cultures.

There's a real scarcity of 'good men' and it's killing us.

The war on women is a war on earth.

The patriarchy is killing our *Spiritual Authenticity*.

I'm not telling you that you need to go against the grain to be considered authentic but you do need to learn to speak from your heart. Even when you know others will have something to say about it. It's not easy at first, but I can tell you it does get easier. Speaking your truth will encourage you to live it too.

It's always obvious to me when someone hasn't made a personal choice grounded in their sovereignty and intuition. If you need validation or approval to feel grounded in your decisions, then it didn't come from a place of intuition or sovereignty.

You can't be *Spiritually Authentic* without a well-resourced nervous system as without it, you will say yes when you really want to say no. This is you admitting that you value others opinions over your own. You will censor and silence yourself to avoid paying the social consequences of that.

Without sharing your truth, you will never take the required risks to create the life you dream of.

If the last few years have taught us anything, it's that if you were living under obligation, you will have had a complete identity crisis.

Life becomes so much easier when we allow our soul to speak for us, from us. Let yourself change, don't meet her with stagnation or hesitation. Let the shift happen because she who meets you on the other side, will be much truer, more honest, more YOU. When you have a moment of doubt- just keep going! Don't look back as the old you will be a shadow of you at this point. Don't outsource your power, worth or integrity. It literally takes no effort to be your authentic self.

Your spirituality is unique to you. You do not need to be placed inside a box with others. You get to choose what you celebrate in life. You choose what your truth is. So make no apologies for it.

Upon speaking and living in truth, you will find your way to your 'soul contract' much easier.

Your 'soul contract' is an agreement that you enter into pre-birth. Before this is decided, you will be asked which lessons are needed to learn in this life and you will be sent with a mission. This is in essence to help the development of the soul. To allow the soul to progress to its next level of consciousness.

Once you understand what you are here for, what you have been selected to bring to the earth, everything begins to make sense. You no longer feel lost or confused about life. Instead you feel certain, secure and determined.

In order to live with purpose of your soul contract, you must embody authenticity. You cannot live your truth if you daren't speak it. You mustn't be afraid of other's projection or backlash.

When you listen to your spiritual gift, something happens within. It's like you evoke a 'Hell Yeah' type of energy. If you commit to going deeper, it guides you to follow your calling.

One incredible way to discover clues about your soul contract is to connect with your past lives.

I'd had a *'past life'* reading many years before, when I was around twenty-four. Although it wasn't anything intense or transformational for me, as it was just a case of listening to what the medium picked up on. It was still very interesting and I could understand a lot of it in today's life.

For example; he told me that I was a French girl in the late 1800's. I came from a very poor family and had to turn to prostitution to keep us from drowning in poverty. (I can't relate to that part, but can the fact I'm very resourceful)

He said that I spent my days sitting by the river watching the swans as I had an infatuation with them. Ok, so this part is *very* accurate! I do this today! I adore going to see the swans, I even feed them by hand if I see them at a park.

He went on to say that I wanted to become an artist and had great talent, so I used the prostitution to pay for my place in college. I went onto become a great artist and became rich in wealth because of it. I got my family out of financial trouble and nobody in the family were poor again.

So what I really took from this was that he was telling me I would do anything for my family, I was able to put the trauma to the side in order to create a new life, one I really desired. I was a dreamer, a creative and broke a generational curse- poverty.

I can relate to all of this in my current life.

This developed a desire to want to learn more about my past lives, so I went on to do my own past life regressions and also trained to become an Akashic Records Practitioner. Meaning I could help others learn their soul contracts through visiting past and future lives.

Having a past life regression is so valuable in connecting the dots of the main message.

It was upon doing my own that I discovered that in three previous lives, I played the same role in every single one. I was a leader, a soul who was here to teach and lead the way with my message. In each life I would take a stand against society's beliefs and open up the minds of the people so they could consider other ways of living. I was a messenger of light, a guide, I had a strong purposeful mission.

In one life (what I believe to be my first life) I was spreading a message. I had a message to share to show people there was more to life than meets the eye. In this position I was punished, I was beaten and people threw stones at me. But I didn't back down.

In another life, I was a woman in the 1600's who watched her child die. I wanted to leave my husband but it was hugely frowned upon. I did it anyway. I went on to fight for women's rights.

I could see that I was already living out my purpose in this life. I was on the right path. My soul contract made complete sense to me now. It wasn't necessarily that I was here to heal the world with my messages from spirit. That was only part of it.

It was that I was here to break down barriers, to help women connect with themselves on a soul level.

Now, I had already transformed my life since connecting with my higher consciousness. I had met the man I would go onto marry. I had started my own business. I had created my children. I had healed my body through the power of trauma healing.

I had even begun to set intentions for spirit to help me meet more like-minded friends. Women who I could talk openly with, who weren't out to benefit from my gift. Who just wanted to be my friend. Which they went on to provide me in the form of clients that went on to be my best friends.

I was really enjoying my life, but I still knew there was more I needed to know.

This was when I was called to teach.

CHAPTER 8

Spiritually Authentic

When I was five I decided I wanted to be a teacher. My very first primary school teacher Mrs Taylor was so kind and patient with me that she was my very first role model. She would have been in her seventies and she always sat with me when I was the last one in the canteen eating dinner. I was always so slow at things. There was nothing wrong, I just liked to take my time with everything.

I soon changed my mind about becoming a teacher in a school environment, but the thought of 'teaching' always stayed with me.

In jobs, I would always end up teaching somebody something, or be asked to train the newbies.

So during that last two years of upheaval and spending a lot of time pondering my future quests, it was no wonder a download came to me.

Spirit were telling me that now was the time to teach. The world needed my gifts now more than ever. I knew they were right.

So I put the news out there that I was going to start my own course to teach any women how to unlock their gifts, if they felt ready. I made a point that they should only sign up if they were serious about it. I didn't want time wasters. I needed women who had that hunger inside of them.

I had fourteen women immediately sign up, no hesitation.

I wasn't expecting that!

Still the odd moments of imposter syndrome creep in from time to time. I didn't plan out the course rigidly. I had a rough idea of what I would do and it worked well.

Very well.

Things soon developed, I was being asked to teach others and coach women in their businesses.

Fast forward two years and I now have two memberships, my shows are sell-outs, I have celebrities message me and I am the happiest I have ever been. All along my purpose was right in front of me.

I was supposed to teach.

But not until I had experienced the events that I had to go through. I had to endure heartache and trauma, so that I could use it in a way that brought teaching into the world.

I turned my pain into my power.

I also qualified as a *Fertile Body Method Practitioner* to work alongside women experiencing infertility.

My life has totally transformed from the twenty-one-year-old having a breakdown, wanting to give up her opportunity of life. I now help so many women to reap that same transition.

What do you stand for? What do you want to be known for?

Being authentic means **knowing who you are and the purpose of your existence**. It means you are deeply rooted in your beliefs, desires, and values and are living them out each day. It means you have taken yourself to the next level, having defined what is most important to you.

You have up-levelled.

You have taken yourself from living a 3D experience to a 5D adventure. That's the reality and magick of this development.

Once you are living spiritually authentically, anything becomes possible for you. Your gifts can give you so much as long as you embrace them wholly and with the upmost truth.

Now you know the *Five Steps to Spiritual Connection*, I want to give you a few tasks to help you along your journey.

Task One

By thinking about your limiting beliefs, I want you to answer these questions in a notebook:

What does holding this belief cost me?

Is it my belief, or does it belong to somebody else? I.e. Parents, friends, partners.

Who are the people I spend the most of my time with and how do they influence the way I think and feel?

The point of these questions is to enable you to see why you have been unable to move forward in life with your gift so far. Or why you are only so far along and may be facing an obstacle.

You may want to list all the times you remember where you have felt hurt, betrayed or humiliated. Alongside each memory, write the emotion you felt at this time. You will decide in this moment to release the limiting belief this memory created for you and instead replace it with a new positive affirmation.

Words are powerful. We listen to our own inner voice more often than anybody else's voice. We can use this weapon as our power or our kryptonite.

I have listed here some of my most used affirmations:

I am in charge of my own energy. I choose how I feel.

When I am feeling overwhelmed, I allow myself space to pause, breathe and reflect.

I am free of my limiting beliefs. Although my parents and society pushed their beliefs on to me from a young age, I have the final say over what I believe as an adult.

The only beliefs that I entertain are those that are self-nurturing, self-loving and will help me grow as an individual.

I know that I can achieve all I want just by being myself.

Today I choose to release any lingering self-doubts.

Task Two

A great task to build on your trust with spirit is to ASK them for a GIFT.

Let's not get carried away here, this isn't going to necessarily be an extravagant physical gift.

What you need to do, is find a quiet space and moment. I want you to focus on nothing but your third eye. This can work best when laying down. Tilt your eyes slightly back and focus on the colour you see. This might be white, golden or lilac.

I want you to count down in your mind, still focusing on your third eye, from ten. Once you reach one, you will be shown a gift in your mind's eye. This could be anything from a purple monkey to a china cup! What the object is, isn't the goal here.

It may take a few days for you to receive your gift. You may see your gift whilst scrolling through social media, you may come across it whilst sitting in your car. You won't know how or when it will arrive, but it will. This is a task to teach you to have trust in spirit. To believe and accept that they will grant you your gift. This will build on your connection. If you are on social media, I invite you to come into my online community to share your gift with us.

Meditation

This guided meditation is only a short version to help you memorize it and even tweak it to suit you if you prefer. It is for you to meet your spirit guide.

Sit comfortably

Feet firmly on the ground

You are going to count down from ten.

With every number, focus on your breathing. Soft and slow breaths. In and out

10, 9, 8

You are getting more and more comfortable

7, 6, 5

You can see a white light flowing through your body. You feel safe and secure

4, 3

You are becoming very aware that you are not alone

2, 1

You open your eyes and see the sun beaming down on your face through the treetops

You sit up and take some steps forwards

You are very aware that you are in a beautiful forest. Surrounded by the sounds of bird song

Go for a walk

As you wander around the forest, you see a waterfall and a bench beside it

Go to the bench

As you sit down you sense a presence beside you

This is your guide

(You may see them, you may only sense or hear them)

Allow yourself to communicate

Ask your guide for their name. Take in anything you feel whilst sitting there. You may see obvious physical traits, you may see colours

Ask them what it is that you need to know

Ask them for guidance on what is playing on your mind

(Spend a few minutes together, building on your connection)

It's time to say good-bye to your guide. As you stand up, head back to the spot where you woke.

As you lay back down, I want you to count back down from ten

10, 9, 8, 7, 6, 5, 4, 3, 2, 1

Once you are back to consciousness, grab a notepad and pen and write down everything that you remember.

The Clairs

There are many ways to work at strengthening your *Clair senses.*

Exercise One

Choose to spend time with somebody close for a few hours. But do your best to remain as present as possible. This means, avoiding technology, noisy places. You need focus.

On your way to meet them, set the intention to open up. You want to be able to use your *Clair* senses whilst in this person's presence.

Make note during your time together of any physical feelings you sense on your own body. This can be anything from a tickle, a burning sensation or a cool breeze.

When you leave, close down and go and grab a notepad and write down everything you felt. Try not to overthink this. Some things you felt may be your own. But once you have written it down, relay these sensations back to your friend and ask them if there's any relevance. They will confirm for you.

Exercise Two

Choose a trusted person and have them sit in front of you on a chair.

As you stand in front of them, close your eyes and count to ten. Then open them, focusing on this person, look straight towards their head. As you focus on this area, you will see a haze of colour around the outline of their body.

Once you see it, ask spirit to tell you what this colour aura means for this person. You may hear an answer back in your own voice. Trust in what you hear back. Relay it to the person to see if they can relate to the message.

Practising these methods will guarantee you begin to feel more acquainted with your abilities. There is no expiry date that comes with your gift. You can pick up back up whenever you need. The more you do use it however, the more impact it will have.

And Finally...

I hope that I am leaving you feeling inspired and enlightened.

At times, it may feel like you are going three steps forward and two steps back, but nobody said it would be easy. Embracing your spiritual essence can be totally draining at times as you hit brick walls or being to see through new eyes. People will astonish you. Life can switch on you through no fault of your own.

Not everything happens for a reason, but you can make a reason for everything. You get to decide what happens next. You can choose to heal, grow and evolve.

Allowing your third eye to guide you instead of two eyes that can only see so much, is where your transformation begins. You are a soul living a human experience, or so it seems.

You have the power to change that.

Your paradigm of this world relies on you recognising the difference between the man-made ego and the divine soul inside which connects with the universe.

For too many years, life times and generations of women have been and gone through this same transition. You can either pretend to yourself that your gifts can't give you the things I tell you it can. Or you can use this book as a step forward, a step that leads you down a beautiful, sometimes challenging road of new beginnings and miracles.

Be excited to step out of your comfort zone, for the growth it will bring you will be worth it. Everything you desire is on the other side of 'comfortable'.

I want for you to open your middle eye and see the potential available to you. We have a responsibility to share our wisdom to create a new world. One where we are free to be who we are, no questions asked.

By following the steps in this book, you will have all the spiritual tools within your grasp. You can use them for the highest transformation and set new standards for your worthy and beautiful life. My system isn't a 'one-size fits all' though. You can pick the parts that feel the most relevant to you.

What my system will give you is the real guidance you need to become *Spiritually Authentic*. To be the best possible version of you and getting the most from your gifts.

Your gifts are already there. They always have been.

About the Author

JEMMA BROOKES

Jemma is a well-known and loved Psychic Medium and Spiritual Mentor. Her reputation for being down to earth, whilst providing the most unexplainable accuracy in her spiritual work, has resulted in the demand for her courses.

Jemma is a change-maker on a mission to change the paradigm of the way the world views spiritual women. She feels that by helping women to unlock their own gifts, this can create a domino effect for generations to come. She believes by doing this, the world will have more Starseed children embrace their spiritual pathways without prejudice.

Jemma continues to share her life-experiences in order to create a world filled with love and truth.

To find out how you can work with Jemma to step into your spiritual transformation, head to

www.jemmabrookes.com

facebook.com/jemmabrookespsychicmedium

instagram.com/jemmabrookespsychicmedium

References

4. RECOVER

1. https://www.ncbi.nlm.nih.gov/pmc/articles/PMC6116551/
   #CR29

Printed in Dunstable, United Kingdom

68117911R00097